P9-AGM-788

fingerfood

Elsa Petersen-Schepelern **finger**food

photography by William Lingwood

TIME
LIFE
BOOKS

Alexandria, Virginia

TIME® LIFE BOOKS

Time-Life Books is a division of Time Life Inc.

TIME LIFE INC.
President and CEO: George Artandi

TIME-LIFE CUSTOM PUBLISHING
Vice President and Publisher   Terry Newell
Vice President of Sales
and Marketing   Neil Levin
Director of Acquisitions
and Editorial Resources   Jennifer Pearce
Director of Creative Services   Laura Ciccone McNeill
Director of Special Markets   Liz Ziehl
Project Manager   Jennie Halfant

TIME-LIFE is a trademark of Time Warner Inc. U.S.A.

Petersen-Schepelern, Elsa.
Finger Food / Elsa Petersen-Schepelern : with photography by
William Lingwood
          p. cm.
   Includes index
   ISBN 0-7370-2022-9
   1. Appetizers. 2. Hors d'oeuvres. I. Title.
TX740.P4644 1999
641.8' 12--dc21   99-46942
                                   CIP

Books produced by Time-Life Custom Publishing are available at
a special bulk discount for promotional and premium use.
Custom adaptations can also be created to meet your specific
marketing goals. Call 1-800-323-5255.

10 9 8 7 6 5 4 3 2 1

First published in the United Kingdom in 1999 by
Ryland Peters & Small, 51–55 Mortimer Street, London W1N 7TD
Text copyright © Elsa Petersen-Schepelern 1999.
Design, photographs and illustrations copyright
© Ryland Peters & Small 1999.

Printed and bound in China

Author's Acknowledgments
My thanks to my sister Kirsten and my nephews Luc Votan, Zac
Stümer, and Peter Bray for all their help. Thanks also to fellow
cooks, including Clare Ferguson, Rosemary Stark, Sue Holmes,
Tessa Kerwood, Susan Haynes, Ashley Western and Elle Kiss,
Michael Ryland, Fiona Smith, and Sunil Vijayagar for their input,
and to "my" author, Linda Collister, for teaching me about
baking. Particular thanks to Sheridan Lear and Maddy Bastianelli
who helped with recipe testing, to Robin Rout for his design, and
William Lingwood for his beautiful photography.

Notes
Spoon measurements are level.

Uncooked or partly cooked eggs should not be served to the
very old or frail, the very young, or to pregnant women.

Specialty Asian ingredients are available in large supermarkets,
Asian, Thai, Chinese, Japanese, and Vietnamese stores.

Ⓥ Designates recipes suitable for vegetarians.

Designer
Robin Rout
Editor
Elsa Petersen-Schepelern
Assistant Editor
Maddalena Bastianelli
Production
Patricia Harrington
Head of Design
Gabriella Le Grazie
Publishing Director
Anne Ryland

Food Stylists
Sunil Vijayakar
Maddalena Bastianelli
Stylist
Mary Norden
Photographer's Assistant
Briar Pacey
Author Photograph
Francis Loney

Contents

Serve **fingerfood** that's a mixture of prepare-ahead and last-minute assemblies. You'll need 4–6 pieces per person per hour.
But above all, choose recipes that will help to take the panic out of partying!

What kind of party?

The recipes in this book are designed to be served as finger food at a cocktail party. Usually such parties last for 2–3 hours. If you've asked people for a longer time, then you should also serve them one or more substantial dishes.

You can also use the recipes as nibbles to serve with drinks before a dinner party—just choose your dishes well, so you don't fill people up before dinner, or clash with the courses you're serving for dinner. Take care with quantities too—I've often had to wrest the Flat Beans with Hummus from people who've come to dinner, in case they didn't have any room for the main event.

How many people?

The size of your party will depend on the size of your house—or garden—and the capacity of your kitchen. In a small apartment, half a dozen people might be the limit. In a larger house or a garden, the numbers might swell to dozens, or even hundreds (though if you've invited hundreds, I suggest you call in the professionals!).

Recipe choice

Choose 4–6 items per hour—several easy things from the first chapter, then one each from other chapters.

Sweet things, like ice cream and cake, should be served at the end of the party—they signal "finale."

Unless you have a large house, where cooking smells won't invade the party, cook deep-fried items the morning or day before, then reheat in the oven.

Recipe order

Serve treats like oysters, shrimp, or caviar first, with proper fanfare.

In fact, treat your party menu like an ordinary meal. Serve light and fresh things first, such as soups or morsels wrapped in leaves, then more substantial foods like sushi, hamburgers, or bruschetta—to help soak up the alcohol. Follow these with rice, bread, or pastry, then the more substantial dishes of meat or poultry.

Then something light and salady, then savory and cheesey, then sweet. Most people can't drink any more alcohol after sweet things—it's a good way to signal party's end.

One Thing at a Time

Serve just one kind of food at a time. Remember those who don't eat meat, or can't eat the kind you're offering; so include a vegetarian or chicken option.

Waiters and Sous Chefs

Depending on the size of your party, it's only sensible to have helpers—family or friends, professional waiters, or chefs.

Hire them far in advance and brief them well before they start serving. They must know what to do, how you want them to do it, and what they're serving.

Food Facts

How much food?

It depends how long your party will be and how many cooks will be available to prepare the food.

I think that one cook—that's you—can cope with about 8 different dishes, but only if you are able to prepare at least half of them in advance. If you plan to serve more, you'll need help, either from family and friends, or hired from an agency. Prepare each dish on the assembly-line principle, completing one task before beginning the next.

Serve 4–6 items each hour per guest, so for 30 people for 2 hours you need 8–12 different dishes—that's at least 240 items, so plan ahead.

What kind of food?

The best collections of finger foods include a range of textures and flavors to please the guests—plus several different preparation and cooking methods to make life easier for the cook. Include:

• Crunchy things, like fries, chips, or deep-fried spring rolls or wontons.

• Savory, salty things like Anchovy Pinwheels and Spiced Nuts.

• Substantial things to soak up the alcohol, like mini hamburgers and hot dogs, pizza, and brushcetta.

• Creamy things like Leaves with Hummus and Tabbouleh Salad, Mini Bagels, or Blini with Cream Cheese and Smoked Salmon.

• Sweet Things (optional) to bring the party to a close.

Special dietary requirements

Remember some of your guests may have special requirements. Mostly, they will organize for themselves which of your dishes they would like to or can eat. But think of them when you're planning your menu.

• If they're weight-watchers, have pity. Don't make every single thing deep-fried or creamy.

• If some have religious taboos, don't serve too many dishes made with pork, seafood, or beef.

• Some may be vegetarian, so make sure there are several things they can eat (and make sure your waiters know which they are). Vegetarian dishes in this book have been marked with a special symbol after the serving quantity—Ⓥ

• Some may even be vegan—that means no animal products of any kind, including eggs, cheese, or cream. Point them toward vegetable sushi or stuffed vine leaves and have some bruschetta that will suit them.

• Some people have allergies, for instance to peanuts, strawberries, chilies, or shrimp. Most allergic people are alert for foods which may cause problems, but if you know your friends have allergies like these, either leave out that ingredient or make sure your waiters know which foods contain problem elements.

Drips

Finger food must be confined to things that can be eaten in one bite—or two at most.

Above all, it must not be unwieldy—the kind of food that tumbles or drips down people's shirtfronts.

Your guests should be able to hold a drink in one hand and the food in the other. Or perhaps both items in one hand, leaving the other free for talking.

Forward preparation

If you're making many different bite-sized foods, you must plan ahead. Prepare some dishes in advance, freezing some, chilling others, and storing yet others in airtight containers for 1 or 2 days.

Have your oven preheated for about 15 minutes before the party starts so you can reheat some ready-prepared dishes and give a quick final cooking to others. I set mine at 400°F throughout the party.

I also have a collection of electronic timers which beep madly as each item is ready. Then you won't miscalculate and burn the food.

Food safety

When you have a party, you're catering for large numbers of people and storing larger quantities of food than usual.

Remember to keep food preparation areas, utensils, and hands scrupulously clean. Heat and cool foods quickly, so they spend as little time as possible in the danger zone for microbe-multiplication. Do not put hot or warm food in the refrigerator, which should remain below 39°F and above 32°F.

Dry or salty items, such as nuts, chips, capers, or olives are safe, because microbes don't flourish under these intolerable conditions.

When you reheat, do so thoroughly (without burning the food to a crisp). The food should be kept at 145°F or hotter until ready to serve. However, when you serve the food, don't serve it blisteringly hot, or people will burn themselves.

How much food can you fit in your own fridge and freezer? When you're catering for lots of people, you won't necessarily have room for it all. That means you must borrow other people's fridges and freezers—or even rent them.

Party Drinks

How much?

Better too much than too little. Be generous! Most suppliers will let you return what you don't use, so it's always better to allow a little more.

Some people will drink—others won't. And you may not know until they get there! Just remember to have enough for both kinds of guests.

Champagne

My favorite party drink is champagne. For a 2-hour party, allow about ½ bottle per guest, for a 3-hour party, ¾ bottle for each person. That looks after the people who drink more and those who drink nothing at all.

There are 6 glasses in a bottle—or 8 if you're mixing it to make Kir (page 134) or a Champagne Cocktail (page 139).

Serve a light, dry kind—such as Mumm, Cuvée Napa, a cava, or Green Point —it doesn't have to be French.

Wine

Again, about ½ bottle per person. When serving wine, you'll probably find people prefer white, with a few die-hards who don't drink anything but red.

Make sure it's good quality and not so distinctive that people's palates will pall after 2 hours of it.

The ratio of white to red will be different in summer and winter. In summer, allow 3 bottles of white wine to 1 of red, and in winter, make them equal—but you know your own guests.

But let's face it, if you allow 1 bottle per person, you can always serve the leftovers at your next dinner party.

Cocktails

Cocktails are a stylish choice, but limit yourself to 2–3 different kinds—one from the brandy-whiskey family, then another from the gin-vodka group, and one from the hold-onto-your-hat gang: tequila, rum, etc.

If you don't have barmen on hand—and since it's difficult to prepare cocktails in advance—limit yourself to something easy to make. Cocktails can be pretty intoxicating, so many people like to have just one, or possibly two, then move on to another kind of drink.

Garnishes

Order lots of limes and lemons and cut them into slices and wedges in advance, covering them with plastic wrap to prevent them from drying out.

Other garnishes will depend on the drinks you're serving. Olives and lemon zest for Martinis, maraschino cherries for Manhattans, cucumber for Pimms. And mint for Juleps of course.

Spirits

If a person is a Scotch drinker, he (and he's often a he) won't be happy with wine. There are 16 measures in a 750 ml bottle of Scotch or whiskey and other spirits. Three is all most people will manage in a 2-hour party.

It's not necessary to offer every spirit available—the three most popular, Scotch, vodka, and gin, are probably enough, though tequila and bourbon also have their dedicated followers.

Mixers

Mixers should include sparkling and still mineral water, soda water, cola, tonic, ginger ale, and orange, grapefruit, and tomato juice.

Punch-bowl drinks

Big party drinks, which can be prepared or part-prepared in advance, include Planter's Punch, Sangria, non-alcoholic punch, Glögg, or glühwein, and so on.

The very strong ones, like Planter's Punch, contain about the same amount of alcohol as a strong measure of spirits, so cater accordingly.

The lighter, wine-based drinks such as Sangria contain only a little less alcohol than wine itself, so cater as for wine.

Glögg, glühwein, and mulled wine contain spirits as well as wine, though some of the alcohol will disappear when the drink is heated.

Mineral water and soft drinks:

Allow 1 bottle for every 3 or 4 people and provide half still and half sparkling.

The Designated Drivers and other teetotallers will be delighted if you make an effort with their drinks, and even the drinkers will be glad of something fresh when they decide to stop drinking.

Remember—lots of ice!

11

Serving
Ideas

Because finger food is usually an assembly of many small things, how you present them is important. The more attractive the presentation, the more delicious the food will appear.

Throughout this book, we've given you lots of ideas about presentation.

Bite-size containers

Sometimes I have suggested you use bite-sized containers, such as:

• spoons

• paper cones

• waxpaper cups

• shot glasses

• demitasse coffee cups

• Moroccan tea glasses

• toothpicks

• satay sticks and chopsticks.

Foods like crisps and nuts will not only taste better in separate containers, but little twists and cones are more hygienic too, and will save on the washing up.

Serving trays

You will already have a collection of serving trays in your kitchen, so dress them up in lots of ways, with napkins, leaves, linens, and papers.

But be careful—make sure they won't be too heavy to carry, because when they're loaded with food, they're going to be even heavier!

However, though everyone has a collection of plates and trays, they don't usually have enough for a party. So—rent them, borrow them, or improvise, as I have here.

Improvised trays can be made from:

• cane baskets and plates

• wooden chopping boards

• tennis rackets and pingpong bats

• oven racks and cake cooling trays

• cardboard and wooden boxes and their shallow lids (keep any glamorous chocolate boxes any one gives you— they make perfect serving trays)

• bark tubs and even flower pots

• heavy card, folded into box shapes and secured with toothpicks.

Tray cloths

Cover trays with:

• tracing paper

• blotting paper

• folded brown paper

• colored gift papers, but take care that the dyes won't harm the food

• fresh and dried leaves

• tray cloths and table napkins

• linens and hessians, hemmed, torn or scissor-cut.

Your imagination is the only limit!

Countdown

One week ahead

- Order drinks, glasses, ice, ice buckets, and bins for ice, drinks, and rubbish. Most suppliers will let you return any drinks you don't use, and will rent out much of the equipment you need.

- Assemble all your serving trays and buy or make others if required.

- Assemble special serving items, such as paper twists and cones, cocktail napkins, tray and tablecloths, baskets, toothpicks, and bamboo skewers.

- Arrange candles and music.

- Organize kitchen equipment required for the menu you've chosen.

- Prepare dishes to be frozen and cooked from frozen, or thawed and reheated.

Two to three days ahead

- Prepare those items that can be prepared then kept in an airtight container until just before serving.

- Make ice creams, wrap Christmas cake logs in fondant, buy ready-rolled pastry.

- Write final shopping lists, ordering from suppliers where necessary.

One day ahead

- Buy all the food, except the most perishable, such as oysters and shrimp. I prefer to buy salad leaves and herbs the day I want to use them.

- Prepare meats, sauces, and marinades. Marinate meats for skewer recipes and chill overnight, either before or after threading onto wooden skewers (skewers should remain damp until ready to cook).

- Cook recipes such as rare roast beef which can be chilled overnight.

- Prepare basic mixtures for macerated drinks such as Glögg or punch.

- Arrange the room and prepare the bar area, set out glasses, toothpicks, napkins, any cocktail equipment, and (many) corkscrews, champagne cork claws, and other equipment.

- Check drinks are cold. (Chilling large quantities of drinks at the last minute is asking for trouble!)

- Check straws, linen, and napkins.

Morning of party

- Collect foods such as salad leaves, herbs, creams, etc.

- Prepare remaining dressings and salsas (page 36) and any herbs or garnishes (float herb sprigs in a bowl of ice water and cover with plastic).

- Cut up any vegetables needed for recipes and cover with plastic wrap.

- Assemble dishes that are able to stand, such as baby potatoes.

Afternoon of party

- Assemble and cook all dishes except those that require last-minute preparation and cooking.

Two hours ahead

- Begin cooking and assembling food, and assemble dishes such as pizzas that need last-minute cooking.

One hour ahead

- Prepare recipes such as Danish Open Sandwiches. Spread with butter, cut, and chill ready for topping.

Thirty minutes ahead

- Preheat the oven.

- The party should be ready to go and first dishes ready to serve. Draw corks from still wines. Prepare the materials for cocktails. Sit down!

When the first guest arrives

- Pull the champagne corks and take the coats. Serve cocktails and champagne.

13

Who said party food had to be difficult and complicated? This chapter, **spoons, cups, and quickies**, shows that simple but delicious ingredients, simply served, can taste wonderful and look spectacular. And they make life easier for the cook.

Smoked Salmon Brochettes

This simple idea can be prepared in the morning, covered with plastic wrap and refrigerated until just before serving (it will taste better if you let it come back to room temperature first).

8 oz. smoked salmon (about 10 slices)

finely grated zest of 2 lemons

freshly cracked black pepper

Makes about 30

Cut slices of smoked salmon lengthwise into long strips, about ½ inch wide and about 4 inches long. (Most slices give about 3 strips.) Carefully thread the strips onto toothpicks.

Arrange the loaded sticks on a serving platter and sprinkle with finely grated lemon zest and cracked black pepper.

Ice-Cold Prairie Oysters

Prairie Oysters are usually regarded as a hangover cure—but take away their medicinal nature, and replace the egg yolk with a real oyster, and they are utterly delicious! Serve this as a canapé-cum-cocktail when people first arrive at the party. Make sure all the ingredients are ice-cold and the vodka has been in the freezer.

3 cups tomato juice

2 cups ice-cold vodka

juice of 6 limes or 2 large lemons

a dash of Tabasco, or to taste

crushed ice

12 freshly shucked oysters

salt and freshly ground black pepper

sprigs of mint (optional)

mini wedges or slivers of lime, to serve

Serves 12

Put the tomato juice, vodka, lime or lemon juice, and Tabasco in a pitcher half-full of crushed ice. Stir well. (To make in advance, omit the ice and chill well. Add the ice prior to serving.)

Put 1 oyster in each of 12 shot glasses, aquavit, or sherry glasses, add the chilled vodka mixture, then top with a mint leaf or lime zest, a little salt and pepper, and a lime wedge speared with a toothpick.

For people who don't like oysters, omit the oysters and serve the tomato mixture as a Bloody Mary.

Variation: Before you start, rub a lemon wedge around the rim of each glass, and press the rim into a saucer of salt, just as if you were making a Margarita.

17

Ever since I saw this idea in a food magazine, I've served many different things in **spoons**, from caviar to ice cream. It always looks just fabulous.

Spoonfuls of Caviar

A spoonful of caviar is incredibly luxurious and a rare treat for most of us. Serve it early in the party, perhaps first-off, with a shot glass of ice-cold vodka. Champagne or white wine is also a good choice!

Unless you're very rich, confine this spectacular dish to very small gatherings! One small 2 oz. can of caviar will serve 8 people. Beluga is sold in a blue can, followed by Oscietre in yellow, and Sevruga in red. Though Beluga is the most highly regarded, the slightly less expensive Sevruga is probably better for a party.

Remember—never serve caviar in a metal spoon. Use bone, wood, glass—even plastic.

2 oz. can of caviar or salmon keta

Serves about 8

Using a plastic teaspoon, carefully take one spoonful out of the can, without breaking any of the eggs.

Put into a serving teaspoon, smoothing it carefully (remember—no metal!). Repeat until you have enough for each guest. Arrange the spoons on a plate (rectangular is better) and serve.

Variation: Other kinds of caviar are also delicious. Try Salmon Keta, Trout Eggs, Tuna Eggs, Lumpfish, Mullet, Sea Urchin, or American Caviar.

For larger gatherings, other dishes can be served on spoons—or try them in leaves (pages 78–81).

Spoonfuls of Goat Cheese ⓥ

In a small bowl, mix 1 cup goat cheese, ½ cup cream, 1 cup snipped chives, salt, and freshly ground black pepper.

Using a melon baller or the smallest ice cream scoop dipped into boiling water, scoop out balls of the mixture and place in a teaspoon or Chinese porcelain soup spoon. Arrange the spoons on a platter and serve.

19

Spoonfuls of Spicy Thai Salad

Mix 2 cups cooked crabmeat in a bowl with 2 teaspoons lime juice, 2 teaspoons fish sauce or soy sauce, 1 teaspoon sugar and 2 chopped red chilies. Serve as above.

Spoonfuls of Keta, Gravlax, and Chives

Mix 8 oz. gravlax (cured salmon), finely chopped, with ¼ cup snipped fresh chives. Put spoonfuls on the serving spoons, flatten slightly, then top with a small pile of keta (salmon caviar) or flying fish roe. A little crème fraîche or sour cream between the layers is also delicious.

Gazpacho

An unusual gazpacho with clear, bright tastes. Make sure all the vegetables are ice-cold.

4 yellow or orange peppers

1 basket yellow cherry tomatoes, halved, plus 12 red cherry tomatoes, quartered, to serve

2 garlic cloves, crushed, with salt

3 mini cucumbers

6 radishes

6 scallions, white and green, sliced

1 bunch chives, snipped (optional)

tiny sprigs of mint or basil

salt and cracked black pepper, to taste

Serves 24 Ⓥ

Peel and core the peppers with a vegetable peeler and chop the flesh into a blender. Add the yellow tomatoes, garlic, and 3 cups crushed ice and blend to a vibrant yellow purée. Chill until ready to serve.

Cut the cucumbers in half lengthwise and scrape out and discard the seeds. Thinly slice the cucumbers and radishes diagonally on a mandoline. Slice the scallions diagonally crosswise.

Put the purée (thinned a little with water if necessary) into small cups, glasses, or waxpaper cups, add pieces of cucumber, radish, red cherry tomato, and scallion. Sprinkle with the herbs, sea salt, and cracked black pepper, then serve.

Pea Soup with Mint

Freshly shelled peas are best— you can cheat with frozen ones (but cook them for a shorter time). For the harassed party host, here's a microwave-blender version.

1 tablespoon olive oil

8 slices pancetta (as thin as possible)

3½ cups shelled fresh peas

4 cups boiling chicken stock

sea salt and freshly ground black pepper

mint tips, to serve

Serves 24

Heat the olive oil in a skillet, add the pancetta and sauté until crisp. Remove and drain on crumpled paper towels.

Microwave the peas on HIGH for about 2–4 minutes, or until tender. Transfer to a blender, add 1 cup stock, salt, and pepper. Zap to a purée, then add the remaining stock and blend again. Taste and adjust the seasoning, then add extra stock or boiling water if too thick.

Pour into waxpaper cups, demitasse coffee cups, or heatproof glasses. Serve topped with crisp pancetta and a mint tip.

Note: The soup will thicken as it cools, so make it a little thinner than you want the end result to be.

Sweet Potato Soup

A delicious tropical soup using orange sweet potatoes—use pumpkin instead if you like.

1 onion, finely chopped

2 garlic cloves, crushed

1 inch fresh ginger, grated

2 stalks lemongrass, finely chopped

2 red chilies or 1 tablespoon red Thai curry paste

1 tablespoon lime juice

3 tablespoons peanut oil

1 lb. sweet potatoes (about 2 large)

2 cups canned coconut milk

2 cups stock, chicken or vegetable

salt and freshly ground black pepper

To serve:

finely grated kaffir lime zest

finely sliced red chilies

Serves 24 Ⓥ

Put the onion, garlic, ginger, lemongrass, chilies or curry paste, lime juice, and 2 tablespoons of the peanut oil in a blender or spice grinder (coffee mill) and zap until smooth, in batches if necessary.

Heat a wok, then swirl in the remaining oil. Add the spice paste and cook gently for 5 minutes. Do not let it burn.

Add the sweet potatoes, coconut milk, and stock. Simmer, uncovered, until the sweet potatoes are soft. Transfer to the blender and zap again. Season to taste, reheat if necessary and serve in waxpaper or demitasse cups or heatproof glasses, topped with finely grated kaffir lime zest and sliced red chili.

These **quick assemblies**, are so simple that they don't need much in the way of a recipe, just a few serving ideas.

22

These dishes are invaluable as finger food, because one or more of them can be prepared earlier, covered to keep them moist, then brought out between your more time-consuming efforts.

Oysters on Ice

There is nothing better than a plate of super-fresh chilled oysters still in their liquid.

Arrange them on a plate of sea salt and seaweed, and prepare them properly without any specks of shell, and with the oyster properly detached from the shell. Add lemon wedges if you like (though I think oysters are better absolutely plain).

Serve with chilled champagne or white wine, but never ever with whiskey!

Mini Eggs with Dipping Spice

Quail eggs are just incredibly pretty—but quite difficult to peel. You have to pierce the shell, then the very tough membrane under the shell. If unavailable, use small hen eggs, halved, instead.

1 dozen quail eggs or 6 small hen eggs

2 tablespoons celery salt, salt mixed with pepper or dried crushed chilies, Japanese 7-spice, furikake seasoning, or a dip of your choice (pages 36–37)

Serves 12 Ⓥ

Put the eggs into a small saucepan of cold water and bring to a boil. Simmer for 3 minutes for quail eggs and 5 minutes for hen eggs, then turn off the heat, drain immediately and fill the pan with cold water.

Tap the shells all over, then peel under running water. If using hen eggs, cut them in half lengthwise.

Arrange on a small serving plate with a dish of celery salt, spiced salt, furikake seasoning, or a dip.

I like to put one or two back into a small base of shell because the shells are so pretty. Try not to include any unshelled eggs, because there's always someone who's not seen them before and will try to eat the whole egg, shell and all!

Variation: Shell all the eggs and serve in a basket, half-and-half with fat black olives.

Chargrilled Indian Cheese

Other cheeses, such as Italian provolone or farmer's cheese, can be used for this dish, but the original uses Indian paneer cheese. The recipe is a favorite from my friend Usha, a great cook, who lives in Agra, the city of the Taj Mahal.

peanut or mustard oil or ghee (clarified butter), for brushing

1 lb. paneer*, provolone, or farmer's cheese, cut into ¾-inch cubes

Makes about 8 Ⓥ

Brush a stove-top grill-pan or skillet with oil or ghee. Briefly char-grill or pan-fry the cubes of cheese until lightly browned on all sides. Serve warm or cool.

*Note: Paneer is sold in Asian and Indian markets. To make it yourself, put 4 cups full cream milk in a saucepan, bring to a boil, stir in 2 tablespoons fresh lemon juice and 2 tablespoons plain yoghurt. When the milk curdles, pour it into a colander or strainer lined with cheesecloth and let drain for 3 hours. Cover with cheesecloth, put a plate on top and a heavy food can on top of that. Chill for 4 hours or overnight until the cheese hardens a little (the longer you leave it, the harder it will be), then invert and cut into cubes. Drain on a clean cloth, then use.

Flat Beans and Hummus

This dish is so simple—and incredibly popular. I have served it with drinks before dinner parties and people have loved it so much they've almost had no room for the rest of the food!

1 lb. flat beans or runner beans

1 cup hummus, either store-bought or homemade

To serve (optional):

2 teaspoons extra-virgin olive oil

freshly cracked black pepper

Serves 6–8 Ⓥ

Top and tail the beans, then cut them diagonally into 1–2-inch sections.

Spoon the hummus into a small bowl and swirl the top. Sprinkle with olive oil and pepper, if using.

Put the bowl on a serving platter with the beans beside.

Shrimp

make superb finger food. Serve medium-sized ones, peeled and deveined, with just the tail fin intact to act as a handle.

Plunged Shrimp with Chili Mojo

An easy recipe with one simple requirement—perfect shrimp. Test before you buy: texture is everything—they must be firm with tightly curled tails.

1–3 cooked or uncooked shrimp per person, depending on size

Chili Mojo (page 37)

Serves 1

If using uncooked shrimp, insert a toothpick at the neck of each shrimp and pull out the dark vein.

Bring a large saucepan of well-salted water to a boil (you can also add a sheet of kombu seaweed, removing it just before boiling point). Plunge in the shrimp and cook just until the flesh is opaque (about 3 minutes, depending on the size of the shrimp).

Remove with a wire basket or slotted spoon and plunge immediately into a large bowl of ice water to stop the cooking (don't leave them there too long, or you'll wash away the flavor). Remove and chill over ice.

Cut off the heads and remove the shells and legs, but leave the tail fins intact (keep the heads and shells in the freezer and use to make bisques or other seafood soups).

Put the shrimp on a plate or tray with a bowl of Chili Mojo and serve.

Great Caribbean vegetables make superb **chips**. Make them with one or all of the following fruits and vegetables.

My absolute favorite is plantain, the cooking banana just packed with fiber (if you can't find plantains, use green bananas). Cook as many chips as possible, because they're eaten almost as fast as you can make them. You can cook these early in the day and keep them in an airtight container until ready to serve (they will keep for up to 3 days, but seem to lose a little crispness each day). Always try to use a good-quality oil such as peanut, sunflower, or corn oil—those labeled "vegetable oil" often have a mix of oils, some very cheap and often over-refined.

Plantain Chips

6 plantains, green if possible, or yellow, but not black, or 12 green bananas

sunflower oil, for frying

To serve, your choice of:

mild chili powder

chili sauce

Serves about 20 Ⓥ

To peel the plantains, cut off the points at either end, then run the tip of your knife down the length of the fruit, just piercing the skin. Do this in 3–4 places. Carefully run your thumbs under the skin, easing it off. (Another way is to soak the slit plantains in warm water for 10 minutes before peeling.)

Using a vegetable peeler or mandoline, cut long lengthwise strips off the plantain. To make thicker chips, as shown, cut diagonally with a knife.

Meanwhile, fill a wok one-third full of oil and heat to 375°F. (I prefer a wok because you're not wasting lots of extra oil in the corners.) Alternatively, fill a deep-fryer with oil and heat to the recommended temperature.

Add the plantain strips in batches and fry until crisp and golden. Remove with a slotted spoon and drain on crumpled paper towels.

When all the chips are cooked, serve immediately, or let cool and transfer to an airtight container until ready to use.

To serve, sprinkle sparingly with chili powder (don't make it too hot—some people won't like it) and serve in twists or cones of paper.

Alternatively, place on a serving platter with a dish of chili sauce.

Caribbean Chips

Wonderful chips can be made with other starchy vegetables such as sweet potatoes, pumpkin, yams, or parsnips.

Your choice of:

about 1 lb. white or orange sweet potatoes (shown)

about 1 lb. yams, such as eddoes, yellow, coco, or Ghana yam

about 1 lb. pumpkin, seeded but unpeeled

about 1 lb. parsnips

sunflower oil, for frying

spices such as cumin, mixed spice or Thai 7-spice, to serve

Serves about 20 Ⓥ

Finely slice the vegetables on a mandoline, cutting them into narrower strips if necessary.

Fry as in the previous recipe, drain on crumpled paper towels, then sprinkle with spices and serve.

Variation:

Eggplant Chips Ⓥ

Deep-fry finely sliced eggplants (shown left) as in the previous recipe, but at 350°F for about 10 minutes, taking care they don't burn. Don't cook too quickly, or the chips will drink up too much oil. Remove with a slotted spoon and drain on crumpled paper towels, as in the previous recipe. If not crisp, increase the heat to 375°F and fry for 30 seconds longer. Drain again and serve sprinkled with sea salt flakes.

Oven-Baked Tomatoes

I think sun-dried tomatoes are rather leathery in texture and overwhelming in flavor, except when used to make pesto. However, if you oven-bake fresh tomatoes until they've collapsed, they are wonderful as toppings for bruschetta and pizza. If you keep roasting them until they're half-dry, they make a delicious if less crunchy addition to the chip repertoire.

12 small tomatoes (the next size up from cherries) or mini plum tomatoes

sugar

sea salt

2–3 garlic cloves, cut into fine slivers (optional)

Makes 24 Ⓥ

Cut the tomatoes in half crosswise and cut out the dense core with a small, sharp knife. Arrange apart on baking trays. Top each half with a pinch of sugar and a few flakes of sea salt. Push 2 fine slivers of garlic, if using, into the seed section of each tomato half.

Roast in a preheated oven at 400°F for about 1 hour. Test after 30 minutes and 45 minutes. When collapsed and browned but still soft, they can be used as a topping for pizza and bruschetta, or served as a vegetable.

Cook for about 15 minutes longer and they will have dried out enough to be served as a nibble, as shown.

Everyone
loves
traditional
**fish and
chips**
turned into a
mini serving
for a party.

The secret to making perfect French fries (chips) is to twice-fry them. This is just as important for these super-fine fries cut on a mandoline. If you don't have a mandoline, cut them very finely into matchstick lengths.

6 large potatoes, cut into matchsticks

1 lb. salmon fillet, sliced in half lengthwise, then crosswise into ⅓-inch wide strips

sunflower, corn, or peanut oil, for frying

sea salt

Tempura batter:

5 tablespoons cornstarch

5 tablespoons all-purpose flour

1 teaspoon baking powder

5 teaspoons sunflower, corn, or peanut oil

¾ cup club soda or beer

Serves 20

Assemble all the ingredients for the tempura batter, but do not mix it.

Fill a wok one-third full of oil and heat to 375°F. Alternatively, fill a deep-fryer with oil and heat to the recommended temperature.

Add the potato strips in batches and fry for about 2 minutes until cream-colored. Remove with a slotted spoon and spread out to drain on crumpled paper towels. When all the strips have been fried, reheat the oil and fry them again until crisp and golden. Drain on crumpled paper towels and keep them warm in the oven. The fries should be so crisp that they rustle together.

Skim the oil and reheat to 375°F.

Put a large bowl to the left of the wok (if you're right-handed) and a serving platter lined with crumpled paper towels to the right. Have the fish to the left of the bowl. Put the batter ingredients into the bowl and mix quickly with chopsticks, leaving as lumpy as possible, and with a rim of flour left unmixed around the bowl.

Using a pair of long chopsticks or tongs, dip each piece of fish quickly into the batter then place gently in the hot oil. Fry until golden, then remove and drain on crumpled paper towels.

To serve, put a pinch of the fries into each container (in this case a twist of newspaper lined with waxpaper) and add a piece of tempura fish. Make sure all the ingredients are lined up vertically, so people don't drop any on the floor.

Serve immediately, sprinkled with sea salt. You may need to reheat them a little—put them in the oven, in the paper cones, and heat with the oven door open for a few minutes. No longer or they will get too hot (and the paper may burn).

Yes, I know you can buy **toasted nuts**, but it's easy to toast your own, and you can add all sorts of delicious spices to them to make them more personal.

34

They look wonderful, too, served in tiny individual cones, dishes, or boxes. People can hold a drink and a cone in one hand and pick out the nuts with the other. It avoids all those anxieties about many hands dipping into the bowl of nuts.

The quantities will vary according to the number of people you have, what else you're serving, how hungry they were to start with, and when in the party you serve them. I think the chips and nuts come early in the party, right after the first drink.

Serve 1–3 kinds of nuts, but serve each kind separately. I think I would break my golden rule of only one kind of food on the plate too; if people can't tell the difference between a peanut and an almond, they're already having a thoroughly good time and won't care.

Your choice of freshly ground or crushed spices, such as:

cinnamon sticks

cardamom

nutmeg

mild chili flakes

sesame seeds

cumin seeds

paprika

ginger

black pepper

grated citrus zest

Thai 7-spice

Japanese 7-spice

Your choice of fresh, raw nuts, about 1 oz. or 2 tablespoons per person, such as:

peanuts

cashews

macadamias

almonds

pecans

1 tablespoon sunflower oil, for roasting (optional)

sea salt flakes

One cup serves 8 Ⓥ

The number one rule is—fresh nuts and freshly ground spices. Break up the cinnamon sticks and grind them to a powder in a spice grinder (coffee mill) or mortar and pestle.

Wipe out the mill, then grind the black seeds from the green cardamom pods (or buy them already podded—if you do it yourself, the seeds can be a little sticky). If using nutmeg, grate whole ones with a nutmeg grater, or on the finest side of a box grater.

To roast the nuts, heat a dry skillet, add one kind of nut and cook, shaking the pan, until they're aromatic and slightly golden. You must stay with them and keep shaking the skillet, or the nuts will burn and be spoiled.

When ready, tip them into a wide, shallow bowl, then sprinkle with salt and one of the spices or citrus zest.

If preferred, you can cook the nuts with 1 tablespoon of sunflower oil, but your guests will love the flavor of dry-toasted nuts and thank you for that tiny drop of oil you saved them.

To serve, drop about 2 tablespoons of the nuts into each paper twist, tiny china bowl, or folded mini box, arrange in a basket and serve.

Like many of the recipes in this book, **dips** are mix-and-match with other recipes.

Mexican Salsa is good as a dipping sauce, on bruschetta, or mixed with chicken and served in baby lettuce leaves.

1 large red chili, halved

1 mango, seeded and chopped

½ papaya, seeded and chopped

1 small red onion, finely diced

juice of 2 limes

juice of 1 orange

2 garlic cloves, minced

2 teaspoons sugar

a pinch of salt

Makes about 2¾ cups Ⓥ

Broil the chili until the skin blisters (not too long, or the flesh will become bitter). Remove, then scrape off and discard the burnt skin and all the membranes. Chop the flesh.

Put all the ingredients in a bowl and stir well. Mash them a little with a fork if necessary.

Eggplant purée or **Baba Ganoush** is one of the greatest dishes from the Middle East, and variations are found everywhere from Poland to Perth.

1 large eggplant

2 fat garlic cloves, minced

½ cup tahini paste

½ cup lemon juice

salt

1 small bunch parsley, finely chopped

Makes about 2¾ cups Ⓥ

Prick the eggplant all over with a fork. Cook in a preheated oven at about 400°F for about 30 minutes*, or until the outside is charred and the inside is soft and fluffy. (Some traditional recipes suggest that the eggplant be charred over an open flame, or under a broiler, but I was taught by a splendid Polish cook, who just put it in the oven.)

Peel off and discard the charred skin, rinsing off any remaining black bits with water. Put the peeled flesh into a food processor with the garlic, tahini, lemon juice, and salt. Pulse to a purée, taste and adjust the seasoning, then transfer to a serving bowl. Sprinkle with parsley and serve warm or at room temperature. The purée may be covered and refrigerated overnight, but return to room temperature before using.

Serve as a dip, on top of pizzas (page 56), with pita bread (page 96), or stuffed into ciabatta pockets (page 84) either alone or with lamb.

*Note: The time will depend on the size and shape of the eggplant. Keep testing.

Variation: Omit the tahini paste and this purée becomes eggplant pesto.

A **Satay Sauce** contains peanuts, so you might like to serve a plain soy sauce dip as well in case some people can't have nuts.

½ cup fresh peanuts or peanut butter

5 dried red chilies

8 small shallots or 1 large mild onion

1 garlic clove, minced

4 candlenuts or 8 almonds

1 stalk lemongrass, finely chopped, or lemon juice

2 tablespoons peanut oil

1 cup coconut milk

2 teaspoons tamarind paste or lime juice

1 teaspoon brown sugar

salt

Makes about 2¾ cups Ⓥ

Put the fresh peanuts, if using, in a dry skillet and toast until brown but not burned. Crush coarsely.

Soak the dried chilies in boiling water to cover for about 30 minutes. Transfer to a spice grinder (coffee grinder) or blender, add the shallots or onion, garlic, candlenuts or almonds, and lemongrass or lemon juice and work to a paste.

Heat the oil in a wok or skillet, add the chili mixture and sauté gently for about 5 minutes, stirring several times. Add the coconut milk and simmer, stirring constantly (keep stirring, and don't cover the pan, or the coconut milk will curdle). Add the tamarind paste or lime juice, sugar, salt, and peanuts or peanut butter. Simmer for 2 minutes, cool a little and serve.

Note: If this sauce sits for any length of time, you may need to thin it a little with hot water before serving.

Spanish and Mexican Chili **Mojos** are a little more liquid than salsas.

Vietnamese Nuóc Cham is a delicious, piquant, salty, spicy condiment used as an all-purpose dipping sauce. Serve it with deep-fried morsels like spring rolls (page 112), wontons (page 114), dumplings, fresh spring rolls (page 90), or dim sum—or any number of everyday dishes.

Rouille, the Mediterranean mayonnaise-style sauce, is perfect with seafood. **Aioli** is made in the same way, omitting the chilies and bread from the recipe below.

¼ cup chopped fresh flat-leaf parsley

1 tablespoon chopped oregano or marjoram

a pinch of salt

a pinch of sugar

3 garlic cloves, minced

grated zest of 1 lime

½ cup freshly squeezed lime juice

1 large red chili, cored, seeded, and finely chopped, plus 1 small red chili, sliced (optional)

Makes about 1 cup Ⓥ

Put the herbs, salt, sugar, garlic, lime zest, and lime juice in a blender and work until smooth. Taste and add more sugar if necessary. Transfer to a serving dish and stir in the chopped chili.

Taste again, and add the extra sliced chili, if using. Chill for 30 minutes to 3 hours to develop the flavors.

---

2 garlic cloves, crushed

1 red chili, cored and chopped

1 tablespoon sugar

½ lime, peeled, quartered, seeded, and chopped

1½ tablespoons fish sauce

Makes about 1 cup Ⓥ

Work the garlic, chili, and sugar to a purée in a spice grinder (coffee mill) or mortar and pestle. Add the chopped lime and any juice and purée again. Stir in the fish sauce and about ½ cup water, then serve in small dipping bowls.

---

3 garlic cloves, minced

2 large fresh red chilies (or dried chilies, soaked for 15 minutes in hot water), seeded and finely chopped

1 thick slice fresh bread, dipped in water, then squeezed dry

salt

2 egg yolks

1 egg

about ⅓–½ cup olive oil

Makes about 1 cup Ⓥ

Put the garlic, chilies, bread, salt, egg yolks, and egg in a blender or small food processor and work to a paste. Gradually add the oil, drop by drop at first, then more quickly, to produce a thick, creamy sauce.

Potatoes
and other
vegetables
make
wonderful
party food—
filling and
delicious and
a treat for
everyone,
not just
vegetarians.

Baby Potatoes

If you can find blue or yellow-fleshed potatoes, use them for this dish—the effect is spectacular.

1 lb. baby potatoes such as Fingerlings, Yukon Gold, or Purple Congo

Toppings:

sour cream and caviar or salmon keta

goat cheese and chives Ⓥ

cream cheese and chilies Ⓥ

avocado and bacon

mango chutney or pickle Ⓥ

red or green pesto Ⓥ

Baba Ganoush (page 36) Ⓥ

Makes about 20

Cook the potatoes in boiling salted water until tender. Drain, then leave in the saucepan with a folded cloth on top and the lid on top of that. Set aside for about 3 minutes until dry and fluffy. Cool a little then cut in half lengthwise.

Peel any with brightly colored flesh, like Purple Congo, or any with damaged skins. Add one of the toppings and serve.

Variation: Bake in a preheated oven at 400°F for about 20 minutes, or until tender. Remove from the oven, let cool for 1–2 minutes, then cut a cross in the top and press the sides together with your fingers. The cross will open into a frothy flower, which can then be topped with your choice of fillings.

Spanish Potato Tortilla

This omelet is one of the simplest and most satisfying Spanish tapas. To serve more people, make several separate tortillas, don't just increase the quantity of ingredients.

1½ lb. potatoes

1½ cups olive oil

salt

6 eggs

2 red peppers, peeled, cored, seeded, and diced (optional)

Makes 12 Ⓥ

Peel and rinse the potatoes, then cut into ½-inch cubes and pat dry.

Heat the oil in a deep, heavy-bottom skillet, then add the potatoes and fry, covered, for about 20–30 minutes, stirring from time to time. The pieces should be softened but not browned.

Remove from the skillet and drain in a colander. Sprinkle with a little salt.

Beat the eggs lightly with a fork. Gently mix in the potatoes and diced pepper, if using.

Pour off the frying oil, then heat a film of fresh oil in the base of the skillet, add the potato and egg mixture, and shake the pan a couple of times. Cook for 2 minutes or until set.

Cover the skillet with a wide lid, then, holding the lid with one hand and the pan with the other, quickly upturn it, then slide the omelet back into the pan. Cook the other side for about 1–2 minutes. Transfer to a large plate and let cool. When cool, cut into 1-inch squares. Serve with toothpicks.

Yunnan Spiced Spuds

A blazingly hot snack discovered by a friend of mine in a roadside food stall in Southwest China—use mild chili powder for more timid palates. Use smallish potatoes, about 1½–2 inches long.

¼ cup chili powder

2 tablespoons salt

2 lb. small potatoes, unpeeled

peanut oil, for deep-frying

Makes about 12 Ⓥ

Mix the chili powder and salt on a plate.

Cook the potatoes in boiling salted water until tender. Drain. Hold a potato in a dry cloth and pull off the skin using the back of a knife. As each one is peeled, roll it in the spicy salt mixture, pressing it into the surface (you must do this while the potatoes are still damp). Set aside.

Fill a wok one-third full of oil and heat to 375°F or fill and heat a deep-fryer to the manufacturer's recommended level. Add the potatoes in batches and fry for about 2–3 minutes, or until golden.

Remove the potatoes using a slotted spoon, drain, then serve on a plate or in a bowl or basket.

Chargrilled Asparagus

Chargrilling produces a delicious flavor, but you can also microwave or steam the asparagus, plunge into cold water, then drain and plunge into ice water. Drain and serve. Freshly grated Parmesan cheese, plain sea salt flakes, aioli (page 37), or chili oil mixed with rice vinegar are all perfect accompaniments.

1–3 asparagus spears per person

olive oil, for brushing

sea salt, for sprinkling

Serves 1 Ⓥ

Brush a stove-top grill-pan with olive oil, add the asparagus and press them down with a spatula. Cook for 2 minutes on each side (they should be barely cooked), then arrange, tips all one way, on a serving plate.

Alternatively, cook in a microwave for about 2 minutes or in a steamer. Test for doneness (they should be quite firm and crisp), steam or microwave a little longer if necessary.

Serve immediately or drain and plunge into ice water to stop the cooking. Drain again, then arrange as before.

When cooled, they can be kept, covered with plastic, for 1–2 hours before serving.

Fresh Medjool Dates with Goat Cheese

1 lb. fresh dates (about 20)

1⅓ cups mild, creamy goat cheese

Serves 20 Ⓥ

Carefully deseed the dates by placing them on the flat side (press down, if there isn't one). Using a small sharp knife, slit the date along the top. Carefully prise out the stone and press the cavity open.

Cut the cheese into 20 equal parts and carefully press the pieces of cheese into the cavity. Alternatively, if the cheese is very soft and creamy, scoop out 1 teaspoon of cheese per date and insert into the cavity. Smoothe. Make sure a petal shape of cheese shows through the top of the date.

Cucumber Canapés

According to a vegetarian friend, this is the nicest canapé she's ever eaten.

Pea omelet:

1 cup shelled fresh green peas

6 eggs

salt and freshly ground black pepper

butter or olive oil, for frying

Cucumber:

1 long cucumber, about 1½ inches in diameter, sliced ¼–½ inch thick

a large bunch of mint

sesame oil, to serve

Makes about 40 Ⓥ

To make the omelet, microwave the peas on HIGH for 2 minutes, or steam for 3 minutes or until tender. Beat the eggs in a bowl with salt and pepper and ½ cup water.

Heat a large, heavy-bottom or nonstick skillet, add oil or butter and heat for 1–2 minutes. Distribute half the peas evenly over the surface, then quickly pour in half the egg mixture until all the surface is just covered. Cook just until the omelet has set, then slide out onto a large flat plate and let cool. Repeat with the remaining peas and egg mixture.

Slice the omelets into squares or circles a little smaller than the cucumber rounds (or cut out with the top of a small glass). Arrange the cucumber slices on a serving tray, top each one with a piece of pea omelet, a mint leaf, and a drop of sesame oil, then serve.

Savory toppings and fillings for **toasts, buns, tarts, and cones** can be used interchangeably with many of the recipes in this chapter, and with others in this book.

Make life easy! Miniaturized **toasts, bruschetta, and smørrebrød** can be finished with store-bought ingredients as well as homemade.

The only thing to remember when using bread or toast as finger food is that the bases should be small and the toppings should stick sensibly, so they don't tumble down people's shirt fronts.

You can serve them in their bread form, but they go stale or soggy very quickly (unless they're Danish, that is).

I think thinly sliced baguettes or ciabattas provide perfectly sized toast, but other kinds can be halved, or cut into shapes with cookie cutters.

Crisp Toasts and Chargrilled Bruschetta

Easy, mini open sandwiches can be topped with ingredients from the list opposite.

1 baguette or 4 small ciabatta loaves, sliced into ½-inch slices

Makes about 30 Ⓥ

To make Crisp Toasts, arrange the baguette slices apart on a baking tray and cook in a preheated oven at 400°F until lightly biscuit-colored. Take care—don't let them become too crisp or they will break when touched.

Remove from the oven and cool on a wire rack. They can be kept in an airtight container for up to 1 week. When ready to serve, crisp them again in the oven for a few minutes.

To make Chargrilled Bruschetta, put the sliced ciabatta or baguette on a stove-top grill-pan or barbecue and cook until toasted and lined.

Bruschetta Toppings

Choose from the list on page 58, plus other toppings, such as:

- finely sliced Parma ham
- Parmesan shavings
- caperberries
- salted anchovies
- cherry tomatoes, halved.

Onion Marmalade

Delicious caramelized onions can be used in lots of ways—on pizzas, in tarts, on hot dogs and hamburgers, or in leaf scoops.

2 lb. onions, preferably red, finely sliced

½ cup olive oil

1 bay leaf

1 tablespoon sugar

a pinch of salt

1 tablespoon red wine vinegar

1 tablespoon crème de cassis

¼ teaspoon ground allspice (optional)

Makes 2 cups Ⓥ

Put the onions, oil, bay leaf, sugar, and salt in a wide skillet over a moderate heat for about 2 minutes. Reduce the heat, cover, and simmer for about 15 minutes until the onions begin to soften. Stir every few minutes.

Add the vinegar, crème de cassis, and allspice, if using. Cook, stirring occasionally, until the onions have become translucent and caramelized, about 15–30 minutes more. Turn gently with tongs from time to time. Remove, cool, and transfer to a lidded container until ready to use. The marmalade will keep in the refrigerator for 1–2 days.

Danish Smørrebrød (Open Sandwiches)

I include these because I'm Danish, and because the Danes thought of these long before anyone decided bruschetta was the best thing to do with sliced bread. The only thing to remember is you need great bread, good-quality butter, and the freshest toppings. Traditionally, smørrebrød are made with halved, rectangular slices of rye bread—but if you cut them in half again, the little squares will make more manageable finger food.

1 square loaf light rye bread (crusts removed if you like), sliced

lightly salted butter, for spreading

Toppings such as:

leverpostej, beetroot (opposite), and parsley

tiny shrimp, lemon zest, and dill sprigs

smoked or poached salmon, crème fraîche, and chopped dill

pickled herring, baby lettuce, and crumbled hard-boiled egg

smoked ham, blue cheese, and chives

Makes about 48

Spread the bread lightly with butter. Cut each slice of bread in half to make rectangles and in half again to form squares. Pile toppings of your choice on the bread and serve as soon as possible. (The butter will prevent the toppings from making the bread soggy for a while, but don't wait around!)

Leverpostej (pâté)

Leverpostej (liver pâté) is a favorite in our family. When we moved to Australia, my mother tried to buy the traditional pork liver. The butcher refused (not fit food for humans!) and made us have lamb's liver. He was right—even Danes like this Aussie version.

1 lb. well-trimmed lamb's liver, skinned, thickly sliced, then chopped

8 oz. bacon, finely chopped

1 egg

1 teaspoon salt

2 teaspoons freshly ground black pepper

2 teaspoons ground allspice (level)

2 anchovy fillets, mashed with a fork

1 tablespoon butter

1 tablespoon flour

1 cup milk

2 large brown onions, finely chopped

Makes about 2 lb.

Grind the liver and bacon separately in a food processor. Mix with the egg, salt, pepper, allspice, and anchovies. Chill.

Meanwhile, melt the butter in a saucepan, stir in the flour and cook for 1 minute. Gradually stir in the milk and cook until thickened. Cool, then stir in the onion. Mix with the liver mixture.

Transfer to a large terrine, cover with foil and a lid, then stand it in a roasting pan. Half-fill the roasting pan with water, then put into a preheated oven at 400°F. Bake for 20 minutes, then remove the lid and foil and bake uncovered for another 20 minutes. When cooked, the pâté will shrink away from the sides of the terrine. Cool, chill until the next day, then serve.

Spiced Beets

The perfect accompaniment for *leverpostej*—and good with other party food in this book. Sterilize the jars by washing in a dishwasher and filling while still hot.

2 lb. small cooked beets (boiled)

1 tablespoon whole cloves

3 cinnamon sticks, broken

1¼ cups white wine vinegar

⅔ cup measured sugar

Makes about 3 jars, 1 pint each

Cut off the tops and bottoms of the beets and slip off the skins.

Slice the beets thinly* and arrange the slices in sterilized preserving jars. Tuck the cloves and cinnamon sticks down the sides.

Put the vinegar, ⅔ cup water, and sugar in a small saucepan, bring to a boil and simmer until the sugar has dissolved. Pour into the jars until the beets are completely covered (make extra vinegar mixture if necessary—the quantity will depend on the size of your jars). Seal the jars immediately and use within 7 days.

*Note: if serving as finger food, slice the beetroot finely on a mandoline or with a vegetable peeler.

Mini versions of bagels, hot dogs, and hamburgers are popular party food. If you can't buy the tiny **bagels, buns, rolls, and muffins,** here are simple recipes so you can bake them yourself.

48

Mini Bagel Rolls

3 cups unbleached white bread flour, plus extra for dusting

1½ teaspoons salt

1 package active dried yeast (¼ oz.)

½ cup lukewarm milk

1 teaspoon sugar

1 egg, separated

1¾ tablespoons butter, melted

vegetable oil, for greasing

Toppings:

sesame seeds

poppy seeds

several baking trays, well greased

Makes 64 mini bagels ⓥ

Mix the flour and salt and dried yeast, in a large mixing bowl and make a well in the center.

Mix the milk in a bowl with ½ cup lukewarm water. Add the sugar and stir until the sugar dissolves.

Lightly beat the egg white. Pour the liquid mixture into the well, then add the melted butter and egg white and mix thoroughly. Gradually work in the flour to make a soft but not sticky dough. If the dough is too dry, add extra lukewarm water, 1 tablespoon at a time. If too sticky, add extra flour, 1 tablespoon at a time.

Turn out onto a lightly floured surface and knead for 10 minutes until soft, very elastic, and smooth. Alternatively, mix for 5 minutes at low speed in an electric mixer fitted with dough hooks. Put the dough in a lightly greased bowl and turn to coat. Cover with lightly greased plastic wrap or a damp cloth and let rise at room temperature until doubled in size, about 1½ hours.

Punch down the risen dough and cut it in half. Cut each half into quarters, then each quarter into 8, giving a total of 64 pieces. Cover with oiled plastic to prevent the dough from drying out.

Roll each piece into a thin sausage shape about 2–2½ inches long. Taper the ends, brush with a little water and pinch together to form neat rings.

As the rings are made, put them spaced apart on the prepared baking trays, cover and let rise as before until doubled in size, about 1 hour.

Bring a large saucepan of water to a boil, then reduce to a simmer. Add the bagels in batches of 6–9 and poach for 15 seconds until they puff up. Remove with a slotted spoon, shake off the excess moisture and return them to the baking trays.

Mix the egg yolk with 1 tablespoon water and brush over the bagels. Leave plain or sprinkle with sesame or poppy seeds.

Bake in a preheated oven at 400°F for 15 minutes, until puffy and golden. Let cool on a wire rack. (While the first batch is baking, poach the next.)

• *Store in an airtight container up to 3 days.*
• *Bag, label, and freeze for up to 1 month.*
• *Defrost at room temperature.*
• *Reheat in the oven at 400°F for about 5 minutes before splitting and filling.*

Mini Bagels

If you can buy mini bagel rolls, by all means do so, but if you can't, the recipe opposite will help. This filling is American Jewish—my English Jewish friend prefers either cream cheese or smoked salmon (not both) and insists they're really called "beigels."

64 mini bagels

1½ cups cream cheese

about 1 cup smoked salmon (lox), cut into small strips, or salmon keta (red caviar)

freshly ground black pepper

Makes 64

Split the bagels and spread with 1 teaspoon cream cheese. Top with a strip of smoked salmon folded into a curl, or a spoonful of keta. Sprinkle with freshly ground black pepper, put the "lid" back on arrange on trays and serve.

Alternative toppings (from a good Jewish delicatessen or gourmet store) include:
- *schmaltz herring*
- *chopped herring and hard-cooked egg*
- *chopped liver and hard-cooked egg*
- *chopped Spanish onion and hard-cooked egg bound together with schmaltz.*

49

Mini Hamburger Buns and Hot Dog Rolls

You may be able to buy mini hamburger buns and hot dog rolls, but just in case you can't here's a recipe—the hot dog buns are specially measured to fit the most common mini sausages and frankfurters.

4⅔ cups unbleached white bread flour

1½ teaspoons sea salt

1 cake compressed yeast (6 oz.)
or 1 package active dried yeast (¼ oz.)

¼ cup unsalted butter, chilled and diced

1–2 teaspoons sugar

1¾ cups milk (lukewarm or cooler), plus extra for brushing

1 medium egg, at room temperature, lightly beaten

Hamburger bun toppings, your choice of:

plain flour

sesame seeds

caraway seeds

fennel seeds

poppy seeds

rolled oats

several baking trays, greased

Makes about 80 buns or rolls Ⓥ

Put the flour and salt (and dry yeast, if using) in a large bowl and rub in the butter with your fingertips to resemble fine crumbs. Stir in the sugar and make a well in the center.

If using compressed yeast, crumble it into a pitcher, add 1–2 tablespoons of the warm milk and mix to a creamy paste. Add the rest of the milk and stir well.

Pour the yeast liquid and the beaten egg into the well. Work in the flour, drawing it in gradually from around the sides of the bowl to make a soft but not sticky dough. If too wet, add extra flour, 1 tablespoon at a time. If too dry, add extra lukewarm milk or water 1 tablespoon at a time.

Turn out the dough onto a floured surface and knead thoroughly for 10 minutes until smooth, very silky, and elastic. Alternatively, work for 5 minutes at medium speed in an electric mixer fitted with dough hooks. Return the dough to the bowl lightly dusted with flour and cover with lightly greased plastic wrap or a damp cloth. Let rise at normal room temperature until doubled in size, about 1½ hours.

Punch down the risen dough, turn out and knead lightly for 2 minutes. Cut the dough in half and use one half to shape hamburger buns and the other to shape hot dog rolls.

Hamburger Buns:

Cut the dough into pieces the size of hazelnuts and shape into balls. Place the balls on the prepared baking sheets so they almost touch each other. Cover and let rise as before, until doubled in size, about 30 minutes.

Hot Dog Rolls:

Cut the dough into pieces the size of hazelnuts and shape into balls. Roll the balls into narrow cylinders, about 1 inch long, then place on the baking sheets so they almost touch each other. Cover and let rise as before until doubled in size, about 30 minutes.

To bake:

To bake, brush the tops with a little milk and sprinkle with the topping of your choice or leave plain. Arrange, close together, in the baking trays.

Bake in a preheated oven at 400°F for 15 minutes until they are well risen, golden, and sound hollow when tapped underneath. Return to the oven for a further 5 minutes if necessary. If they brown too fast or too much, cover with foil.

Remove from the oven, cool on a wire rack, then split and fill as described on pages 52–53.

- *Store in an airtight container up to 3 days.*
- *Bag, label, and freeze for up to 1 month.*
- *Defrost at room temperature.*
- *Reheat in the oven at 400°F for about 5 minutes before splitting and filling.*

50

Party Mini Dogs

A far cry from the ballpark hot dog—these mini morsels are based on the Danish Pölser, the queen of hot dogs.

20 mini sausages, such as frankfurters, chorizos, or merguez

1 tablespoon olive oil (optional)

40 mini hot dog rolls (pages 50–51)

crispy fried onions (optional)

a selection of different mustards, such as American, German, Dijon, wholegrain, and English, and tomato ketchup

Makes 40

To prepare the frankfurters, bring a large saucepan of water to a boil, then remove from the heat. Put all the sausages into the saucepan for about 3 minutes until heated through, then remove with a slotted spoon.

If serving chorizos or similar sausages, heat the oil in a skillet, add the sausages and sauté gently until cooked through.

Meanwhile, reheat the mini rolls in a preheated oven at 400°F for about 5 minutes. Remove and split lengthwise along the top, leaving attached along one of the long sides.

To serve, drain the sausages and cut in half lengthwise. Into each split roll, insert 1 teaspoon crispy fried onions, if using, and ½ sausage. Close the roll, pipe a zig-zag of mustard or tomato ketchup on top of each sausage, then serve.

Mini Hamburgers

Hamburger patties:

2 cups finely ground lean beef

4 shallots or small onions, finely chopped

3 garlic cloves, minced

1 red chili, seeded and finely chopped

1 egg, beaten

a pinch of freshly grated nutmeg

¼ cup fresh white breadcrumbs

salt and freshly ground black pepper

To assemble:

peanut oil, for sautéing

40 mini hamburger buns (pages 50–51)

barbecue sauce or chili sauce

baby salad and herb leaves

10–15 cherry tomatoes, sliced

4 baby onions, finely sliced

40 baby cornichons (gherkins), (optional)

Makes 40

Mix the patty ingredients together. Take 1 tablespoon of the mixture and shape into a round, flat patty. Repeat until all the mixture is used.

Heat a film of oil in a heavy-bottom skillet until very hot, then add a layer of patties, spaced well apart. Sauté for 2–3 minutes, turning half way, until cooked through.

Remove from the skillet, drain on paper towels and keep them warm while you cook the remainder.

To assemble, reheat the buns as in the previous recipe, then split, leaving one side attached. Put a dot of barbecue sauce or chili sauce into each bun, then a salad leaf, a patty, a slice of tomato, and onion ring. Put the lid on the bun and secure with a toothpick and a mini cornichon, if using.

53

Mini Chili Corn Muffins with Pancetta, Avocado, and Cilantro

If you're not a chili fan, leave them out of this mixture—and you can of course use your favorite fillings instead of the one used here.

1⅓ cups yellow cornmeal

1⅓ cups all-purpose flour

1 tablespoon baking powder

a pinch of salt

2 large eggs, lightly beaten

1¼ cups milk

3 tablespoons melted butter, plus extra for greasing

2 large fresh red chilies, cored and finely chopped

3 scallions, white and green, finely sliced

Pancetta, Avocado, and Cilantro

1 tablespoon olive oil

12 thin slices pancetta or finely sliced bacon, cut crosswise into 1½-inch pieces

2 large ripe Haas avocados

lemon juice, for brushing

cilantro leaves

two deep 12-hole mini muffin pans, greased

Makes about 42

54

Put the cornmeal, flour, baking powder, and salt into a large bowl and mix well. Stir in the eggs, milk, butter, chopped chilies, and scallions, mixing until just combined.

Using a teaspoon, spoon the batter into the prepared muffin pans to about two-thirds full. Bake in a preheated oven at 400°F for about 15 minutes until firm and lightly golden. Remove from the oven and transfer to a wire rack to cool.

Grease the muffin pans again, add mixture as before, bake and cool as before. Repeat until all the muffin mixture has been used. Eat warm on the day of baking or store and reheat as listed below.

To prepare the filling, heat the oil in a skillet, add the pieces of pancetta and sauté until crispy. Drain on crumpled paper towels.

When ready to serve, split the tops off the muffins, cut the avocado into ½-inch thick slices and then into muffin-sized wedges. If the avocado is very ripe, scoop out the flesh with a teaspoon. Put 1 piece of avocado in each muffin, top with a slice of crispy pancetta and a cilantro leaf. Put the tops back on the muffins and serve. If the lids are a bit unstable, spear the whole thing together with a toothpick.

To prepare the muffins in advance:
- *Store in an airtight container up to 2 days.*
- *Bag, label and freeze for up to 1 month.*
- *Defrost 20 minutes at room temperature.*
- *Reheat in the oven at 400°F for about 5 minutes before splitting and filling.*

Goat Cheese Butter Filling:
Mix equal quantities of soft goat cheese and butter, roll into a cylinder about ½ inch in diameter and chill until firm. Slice crosswise into disks, then assemble with the pancetta, as in the main recipe.

Cocktail Blini

Blini are the one Russian dish that has migrated around the world to smart restaurants and parties everywhere. They could have been specially designed as finger food in fact—each blin is about 1–1½ inches in diameter, a perfect one-bite snack (or two-bite if you're being dainty!) You can buy cocktail blini in many supermarkets and delicatessens, but usually they're not made authentically with buckwheat flour. Be different!

1 cup buckwheat flour or half-and-half with all-purpose flour

1 package active dried yeast (¼ oz.)

1 teaspoon salt

1 egg, separated

1 teaspoon sugar

¾ cup lukewarm milk

1 tablespoon butter, for sautéing

To serve:

crème fraîche or sour cream

small pots of caviar and/or salmon keta

herbs, such as snipped chives and dill sprigs

about 4 pieces smoked salmon, finely sliced

Makes 24

Mix the flour, yeast, and salt in a bowl and make a well in the centre. Beat the egg yolk with the sugar and ¾ cup warm water and add to well. Mix well, then cover with a damp cloth and let rise at room temperature until doubled in size, about 2 hours.

Beat in the milk to make a thick, creamy batter. Cover again and leave for 1 hour until small bubbles appear on the surface.

Beat the egg white to soft peak stage, then fold it into the batter.

Heat a heavy-bottom skillet or crêpe pan and brush with butter. Drop in about 1 teaspoon of batter to make a pancake about 1 inch in diameter. Cook until the surface bubbles, about 2–3 minutes, then flip the blin over with a spatula and cook the second side for 2 minutes.

Put on a plate in the oven to keep warm while you cook the remaining blini. Don't put the blini on top of each other. Serve them warm.

To serve, top with a spoonful of crème fraîche or sour cream, some snipped chives or dill sprigs, and a small pile of caviar or keta or a curl of smoked salmon.

* *Store in an airtight container for up to 3 days.*
* *Reheat in the oven at 400°F for about 5 minutes.*

55

Filling and delicious, I think **pizzas and pastries** should form the basis of all party menus.

Homemade Pizza Bases

3⅓ cups unbleached white bread flour, plus extra for dusting

2 teaspoons salt

½ cake compressed yeast (½ oz.) or ½ package active dried yeast (¼ oz.)

1 tablespoon olive oil, plus extra for greasing

2-inch plain cookie cutter and several baking trays, well greased

Makes 100 mini pizza bases Ⓥ

Mix the flour and salt (and dry yeast, if using) in a large bowl and make a well in the center. Add 1¼ cups lukewarm water and the oil.

If using compressed yeast, crumble it into a small pitcher, add 2 tablespoons of lukewarm water and blend until creamy. Mix in about 1 cup lukewarm water plus another 2 tablespoons, then pour into the well with the oil.

Gradually work in the flour to form a soft but not sticky dough. If too dry, add extra lukewarm water, 1 tablespoon at a time. If too sticky, add extra flour, 1 tablespoon at a time.

Turn out onto a lightly floured surface and knead for 10 minutes until the dough is very elastic and smooth. Alternatively, work for 5 minutes at low speed in a mixer fitted with dough hooks. Transfer to a clean bowl dusted with flour, cover with greased plastic or a damp cloth and let rise at room temperature until doubled in size— about 1 hour.

Punch down the risen dough, turn out, knead briefly, then roll out to ⅛ inch thick. Using a 2-inch plain cookie cutter, stamp out rounds. Put onto well-greased baking trays, spaced apart. With oiled fingers press out each pizza round to 2¼ inches in diameter.

Add toppings of your choice and bake in a preheated oven at 425°F for 10–15 minutes. Serve immediately.

• *You can also precook the pizza bases at 425°F for 5 minutes, let cool, then store in airtight containers for up to 2 days. Just before serving, top and bake for about 10–15 minutes.*
• *To freeze, cover and freeze for up to 1 month.*
• *Defrost at room temperature for about 15 minutes, then add toppings and bake.*
• *Alternatively, add your choice of topping (excluding cheese), to the uncooked pizzas, bake for 5 minutes, let cool, then freeze.*
• *Defrost at room temperature for about 15 minutes, add the cheese, if using, then finish baking.*

Mini versions of your favorite Italian **pizza** might have been especially designed for partying.

Mini Pizzas

Use "half-baked" pizza bases from an Italian gourmet store and cut out mini rounds using a glass or cookie cutter—or make your own mini bases using the recipe on page 60. The same store can provide a selection of toppings, and you can make others.

4 Italian pizza bases, about 10 inches in diameter or 28 homemade mini pizza bases (page 56)

olive oil, for brushing

your choice of toppings from the list on this page

several non-stick baking trays

Makes 28 Ⓥ

If using Italian pizza bases, cut out rounds using the rim of a glass or a 1¾-inch cookie cutter. Place apart on baking trays. Brush with olive oil and add your choice of toppings. Bake in a preheated oven at 400°F for 5 minutes, or until piping hot.

If using cheese toppings, brush the pizza bases with olive oil and bake for about 3 minutes first, then add the cheese toppings and heat through for about 1–2 minutes until softly melted, but not running away.

Variation: Instead of store-bought pizza bases or homemade pizzas, you can use slices of bread, toasted, then cut out with a cookie cutter or the rim of a glass. I wouldn't use package pizza mix.

Pizza toppings:

Use a selection of Italian ingredients either homemade or store-bought. Don't use more than 3–4 ingredients on each pizza or the flavors will become too complicated.

- Red pesto brushed over the surface, then topped with a curl of char-grilled yellow pepper and half an oven-dried garlic-spiked tomato (page 31) and sprinkled with fresh thyme leaves. Ⓥ

- Bake the bases for 5 minutes, then top with a thick layer of eggplant purée (Baba Ganoush) (page 36), then sprinkle with toasted pine nuts and cracked black pepper. Ⓥ

- Fontina cheese with anchovy and a dot of red pesto.

- Fontina cheese, pancetta strips, and cracked black pepper.

- Chargrilled yellow pepper with roasted baby artichokes. Ⓥ

- Oven-Dried Tomatoes (page 31) with olive oil or fontina and tarragon. Ⓥ

- Char-grilled red pepper with fried fresh sage leaves. Ⓥ

- Anchovies with melted mozzarella and dried oregano.

- Onion Marmalade (page 45) with Oven-Dried Tomatoes (page 31) or cracked black pepper and salt. Ⓥ

- Sautéed mushrooms with Gruyère, gorgonzola, and mozzarella. Ⓥ

- Flaked fresh tuna with scallions and capers.

- Chargrilled, finely sliced eggplant with Oven-Dried Tomatoes (page 31) and herbs. Ⓥ

Tart Pastry Dough

This easy, basic pastry dough recipe can be used to make mini tart shells of many kinds. If you want to make a larger quantity, make multiple batches. Do not simply increase the quantities of ingredients. If you like making dough by hand, by all means use the traditional method. I don't, because preparing for a party is about minimizing time and effort so the excess can be used to make other dishes— and to have fun!

1⅓ cups all-purpose flour

1 teaspoon salt

¼ teaspoon sugar

7 tablespoons unsalted butter, chilled and diced

1 egg

1 tablespoon milk

a deep 12-hole mini muffin pan or barquette (boat-shaped) molds, as many as possible

Makes about 34–36 mini tart shells or 18 barquettes Ⓥ

Put the flour, salt, and sugar into a food processor and pulse to mix. Add the butter and pulse until the mixture resembles fine crumbs. Put the egg and milk into a small bowl and beat lightly with a fork. Add to the food processor and pulse a few times, then process until the dough forms a ball. Wrap in plastic and chill for about 30 minutes or for up to 1 week.

Mini Tart Shells

Knead the chilled dough briefly to soften, then roll out on a lightly floured work surface to about ⅛ inch thick. Cut out rounds, using a 2-inch plain or fluted cookie cutter. Gather the trimmings, re-roll, and cut out more rounds. Cover the rounds with plastic.

Put 1 round into each of the bases of a mini muffin pan and press into the corners to thin the dough around the edges and to push the dough up the sides of the mold. Prick the base of each tart shell with a fork. (Keep the remaining dough covered with plastic.)

Bake in a preheated oven at 375°F for about 15 minutes until lightly golden. Remove from the oven, cool in the pan for a couple of minutes, then transfer to a wire rack to cool. Wipe the muffin pan clean and repeat until all the dough rounds have been cooked.

Fill with your choice of fillings on pages 62–63 and bake as directed.

- *Use immediately or store in airtight containers for up to 1 week.*
- *To freeze, open freeze in a single layer, then transfer to freezer bags, seal, and label and keep frozen for up to 1 month.*
- *To use from frozen, reheat in a preheated oven at 375°F for 5 minutes, cool, then fill.*
- *To cook a filling in the tart shells, from frozen, let thaw at room temperature for about 20 minutes, then fill and bake according to your recipe.*

Barquette Shells

Knead the chilled dough briefly to soften, then roll out on a lightly floured surface to about ⅛-inch thick. Starting in one corner, put a barquette mold face-down onto the pastry. Using a sharp knife cut round the mold leaving a ½-inch edge of dough all the way round. Press the dough cut-out into the mold, trimming the excess neatly. Repeat for the other barquette molds. Gather the trimmings, re-roll and cut out more barquette shapes.

Prick the base of each pastry-lined mold with a fork, then chill for 30 minutes.

Cut out pieces of parchment paper to fit the shells, press into the shells to cover the pastry, and fill with ceramic baking beans or rice. Stand the molds on a baking tray and bake blind in a preheated oven at 375°F for 15 minutes.

Remove the paper and beans and return to the oven for a further 5–10 minutes until lightly golden. Let cool in the molds for 2–3 minutes, then transfer to a wire rack to cool completely.

Wipe the molds clean and repeat using the remaining pastry dough.

- *Store and/or freeze, then thaw, fill, and bake as in the previous recipe.*

Mini Tarts and Barquettes with Three Fillings

Tiny tart shells filled with all kinds of delicious goodies are wonderful to serve at a party. You can buy the shells, but if they're difficult to find where you live, bake using the recipe on page 60. The shells are filled with a basic savory custard, then all sorts of other flavorings are added.

Don't limit the flavorings to the ones described here.

62

Other ideas include:

- Goat cheese with oregano Ⓥ
- Mixed chopped fresh herbs with Parmesan Ⓥ
- Chargrilled red or yellow peppers and black olives Ⓥ
- Smoked salmon with dill
- Cheddar cheese and chopped smoked bacon
- Green peas with ham and fresh mint
- Oven-Baked Tomatoes (page31) with basil sprigs Ⓥ
- Sautéed mushrooms with fresh thyme leaves Ⓥ
- Middle Eastern lamb and pine nuts (page 117)
- Shredded roast chicken, with corn and chili
- Shrimp and scallions.

36 tart shells or 18 barquettes (page 60)

Basic filling:

1 egg

1 egg yolk

1 cup heavy cream

Asparagus and Prosciutto:

2 tablespoons corn oil

6 slices prosciutto, sliced crosswise

1 onion, finely chopped

2–3 oz. asparagus tips

½ cup freshly grated Parmesan cheese

Leek, Feta, and Black Olives: Ⓥ

1 tablespoon butter or corn oil

7 oz. baby leeks, finely sliced crosswise

½ cup feta cheese, crumbled

½ cup black olives, pitted and halved

Blue Cheese, Pine Nuts, and Basil: Ⓥ

½ cup pine nuts

⅔ cup blue cheese, such as dolcellate or blue castello, chopped

2–3 sprigs of basil

freshly cracked black pepper

several baking trays, well greased

Makes 34–36 mini tarts or 18 barquettes

Prepare the tart shells or barquettes. To make the basic filling, beat the egg, egg yolk, and cream together.

Asparagus and Prosciutto:

Heat the oil in a skillet, add the prosciutto and sauté until crisp. Remove and drain on crumpled paper towels. Add the onion and stir-fry until softened and golden.

Meanwhile, steam or microwave the asparagus tips for 1–2 minutes until al dente. Chop into ½-inch pieces.

Divide the onions, asparagus, prosciutto, and Parmesan between the tart shells, then pour in the basic filling mixture. Cook in a preheated oven at 350°F for 10 minutes or until the custard is set and the tops are golden. Remove from the oven, set aside for 5 minutes to firm the custard, then serve warm.

Leek, Feta, and Black Olives: Ⓥ

Heat the butter or oil in a skillet, add the leeks and sauté gently until softened and translucent. Divide the leeks, feta, and olives between the tart shells, then pour in the egg mixture. Cook as for Asparagus and Prosciutto and serve warm.

Blue Cheese, Pine Nuts, and Basil: Ⓥ

Heat a skillet, add the pine nuts and stir-fry until golden. Divide the cheese between the tart shells, add the egg mixture, top with pine nuts and bake as before. Serve warm, topped with basil sprigs and pepper.

- *The tartlet shells and barquette shells can be prepared, stored, and thawed if necessary as described on page 61.*
- *If you store them, recrisp in a preheated oven at 375°F for 5 minutes. Let cool, then fill as in the main recipe.*
- *The filling, except for the egg mixture, can be added up to 3 hours before baking. Add the egg mixture, then bake as in the main recipe.*

Spicy Mini Shortbreads

Sweet and spicy flavors go very well together. These cookies are great by themselves and also with toppings such as goat cheese and Onion Marmalade (page 45), cream cheese puréed with stem ginger and its syrup, or a leaf filling from pages 78–81.

¾ cup unsalted butter, softened

6 tablespoons sugar

a pinch of salt

1⅔ cups all-purpose flour, sifted

2½ tablespoons rice flour or cornstarch

Chili Shortbread:

1 teaspoon chili powder

Ginger Shortbread:

½ teaspoon ground ginger

2–3 pieces preserved stem ginger, finely chopped

2 tablespoons ginger syrup from the jar

Spice Shortbread:

2 teaspoons apple pie spice

several baking trays

Makes about 100 mini cookies Ⓥ

Using a wooden spoon or electric beater, cream the butter and sugar until light and creamy.

If making Chili Shortbread, add the chili powder. If making Ginger Shortbread, add the ground and stem ginger and ginger syrup. If making Spiced Shortbread, add the apple pie spice.

Add the salt, flour, and rice flour or cornstarch and mix to a firm dough.

Alternatively, put all the ingredients into a food processor and mix until the dough comes together. Wrap in plastic and chill for 1 hour or up to 1 week.

When ready to bake, knead the dough briefly to soften, then roll out on a lightly floured surface to about ⅛ inch thick. Using a 1½-inch fluted or plain cookie cutter, or the rim of a champagne flute, stamp out rounds. Gather the trimmings and continue rolling and cutting until all the dough has been used.

Put the shortbread rounds, spaced slightly apart, on the prepared baking trays and bake in a preheated oven at 350°F for about 12 minutes until just golden. Let cool for about 3 minutes then transfer to a wire rack to cool completely.

- *The cooled shortbread can be stored in an airtight container for up to 1 week.*
- *To freeze, layer the uncooked shortbread rounds between sheets of waxpaper. Freeze, transfer to freezer bags, seal, label and keep frozen for up to 1 month.*
- *The uncooked dough can also be frozen for up to 1 month. Thaw in the refrigerator overnight before kneading and rolling.*
- *To bake from frozen, transfer the frozen rounds to greased baking trays and bake at 350°F for 12–15 minutes or until just golden.*

Anchovy Pinwheels

These simple savory cookies are delicious with anchovies, but you can try other variations, such as red pesto or Gentlemen's Relish.

2 oz. canned anchovy fillets, finely chopped

1 lb. puff pastry, either fresh ready-made or frozen and thawed

beaten egg, to seal

several damp, nonstick baking trays

Makes about 60

Put the anchovies in a mortar and pestle, add 1 teaspoon water and mash or grind to a paste. Keep adding water until a smooth brushable liquid results.

Roll out the pastry on a floured work surface to ⅛ inch thick.

Using a dough brush, brush the anchovy mixture all over the surface (not too thick, or the taste will be too strong).

Brush the far edge with beaten egg.

Starting at the edge nearest you, roll up the dough into a sausage about 1 inch thick, and press the egg-washed edge to seal. Chill for 30 minutes.

Cut the sausage crosswise into ⅛-inch thick slices and arrange flat and apart on damp, nonstick baking trays (sprinkle it with water if necessary).

Bake, in batches if necessary, in a preheated oven at 400°F for about 10–12 minutes until crisp and golden. Remove from the oven, let cool for about 3 minutes, then transfer to a wire rack to cool completely.

• The cooled pinwheels can be stored in an airtight container for up to 3 days.

66

Spice-Speckled Cheese Straws

Homemade cheese straws taste better than the bought variety, and are very easy to make.

1 cup all-purpose flour

½ teaspoon salt

1 teaspoon dry mustard powder

½ cup grated Monterey Jack cheese

2 tablespoons freshly grated Parmesan cheese

5 tablespoons butter, chilled and diced

1 egg yolk

juice of ½ lemon

paprika, for dusting (optional)

several baking trays, greased

Makes 36 Ⓥ

Put the flour, salt, mustard, and both cheeses in a food processor and pulse to mix. Add the butter and pulse until the mixture resembles fine crumbs.

Mix the egg yolk and lemon juice in a small pitcher, then pour into the processor with the motor running. Stop mixing when the mixture forms a ball, then transfer to a floured surface and knead briefly to form a ball.

Roll out to a rectangle about ⅛ inch thick. Using a hot, sharp knife, cut into strips ½ inch wide and 3 inches long. Twist into spirals and place apart on baking trays.

Bake in a preheated oven at 350°F for about 10 minutes until golden. Remove from the oven, dust with paprika if using, then cool on the baking tray.

• *The cooled straws can be stored in an airtight container for up to 3 days.*

Variation:
An easy version is to roll out store-bought puff pastry until very thin, sprinkle with freshly grated Parmesan cheese and mustard seeds, then fold over and roll again. Fold over loosely and cut into strips. Twist the strips into spirals and place apart on a greased baking tray. Press the ends down and bake as in the main recipe.

Shortcrust Pastry Cones

Make pastry cones using cream horn molds. You can start from scratch with homemade pastry dough, or use 8 oz. store-bought fresh dough. If you use dough that has been frozen then thawed, remember you cannot refreeze it in its uncooked state.

1 cup plus 2 tablespoons all-purpose flour, plus extra for dusting

a pinch of salt

6 tablespoons unsalted butter, chilled and diced

1 egg yolk (optional)

milk, for brushing

1 egg yolk, beaten with a little cold milk, to glaze

12 cream horn molds and 1 baking tray, greased with butter

Makes 24 pastry cones Ⓥ

Put the flour, salt, and butter in a food processor and blend until the mixture resembles fine crumbs. Add the egg yolk, if using, and 1–3 tablespoons water. Process until a dough forms. Alternatively, rub the butter into the flour and salt using your fingertips, then add the egg yolk, if using, and enough water to form a dough.

On a lightly floured surface, roll out the dough to a 14- x 10-inch rectangle and trim the edges to neaten. Using a sharp knife or a pastry wheel, cut the dough lengthwise into 24 strips, ½ inch wide.

Brush one side of each strip with milk to moisten and wind the strips around the molds, starting at the narrow tip of each mold, overlapping the pastry slightly by ⅛ inch and finishing neatly on the underside (the pastry should not overlap the metal rim of the mold). Put the pastry-wrapped molds on the baking trays so the seam is underneath. Brush with the beaten egg and milk mixture to glaze.

Bake in a preheated oven at 375°F in 2 batches of 12 for 15–20 minutes until golden. Cool for a few minutes, then carefully twist the pastry cones away from the molds and let them cool completely on a wire rack.

- Thoroughly cooled cones can be stored in airtight containers for up to 3 days.
- Alternatively, freeze in a single layer, then transfer to freezer bags, seal, label, and keep frozen for up to 1 month.
- Thaw at normal room temperature for 20 minutes.
- Recrisp in a preheated oven at 375°F for 5 minutes. Let cool, then fill as in the main recipe.

Pea and Potato Curry

Use these pastry cones to serve your favorite savory mixture. Mine is this Indian vegetarian curry— also used for the samosa filling on page 86. Sweet and spicy flavors are good together.

1 lb. potatoes

2 medium carrots, peeled and diced

½ cup shelled peas, fresh or frozen

2 tablespoons corn or sunflower oil

2 onions, sliced

2 tomatoes, chopped

3 red chilies, seeded and finely chopped

1 teaspoon ground cumin

1 teaspoon ground turmeric

a pinch of salt

Makes about 3 cups Ⓥ

Cook the potatoes whole in boiling salted water until half-cooked. Remove with a slotted spoon, add the carrots and fresh peas, if using, and part-cook them in the same way. Drain. Holding the potatoes in a cloth, pull off the skins and dice the flesh.

Heat the oil in a heavy-bottom skillet, add the onions and sauté until softened and translucent. Add the potatoes and sauté until lightly golden. Add the tomatoes, chilies, cumin, turmeric, and salt and stir-fry for about 2 minutes. Add the part-cooked or frozen peas and carrots and stir-fry until tender.* Spoon into cones and serve.

*Note: The curry can be prepared to this point, cooled and reheated before serving. Potato curries do not freeze successfully, but this one tastes even better when prepared the day before and reheated.

Perfect with finger food, **leaves and seaweed** add crunch and flavor as well as natural wrapability to other savory ingredients.

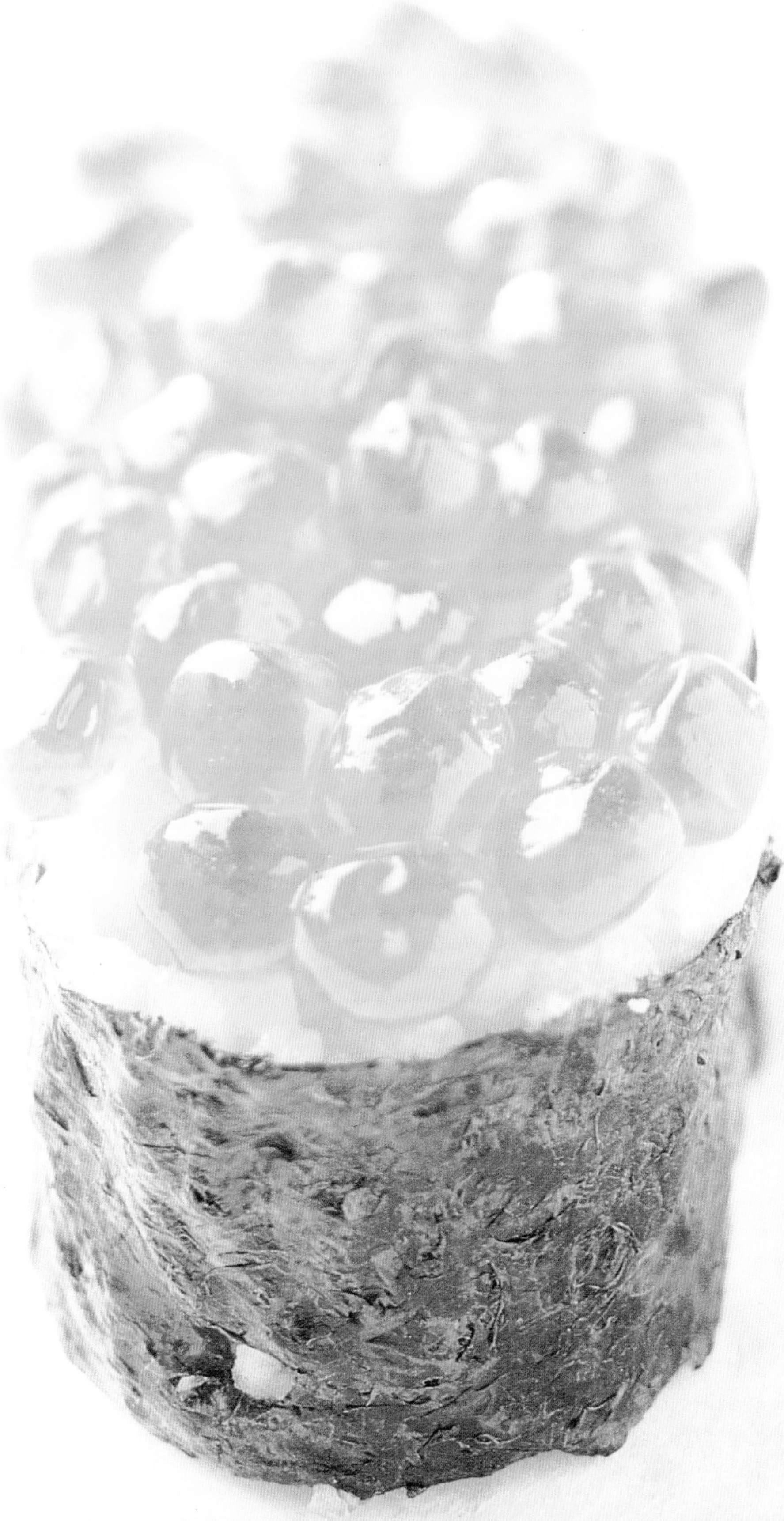

Everyone loves **sushi**, and the homemade kind tastes much more delicious than the store-bought variety. It's also very easy to make.

72

The major requirement is the right kind of rice— aromatic, Japanese sushi rice that sticks together inside the seaweed. Sushi rice is sold in large supermarkets, specialty food stores, and Asian markets, which also sell special sushi fillings. For rolling, use a sushi mat (sold in many supermarkets) or an ordinary bamboo placemat.

Sushi Rice

2 cups sushi rice

Sushi vinegar:

⅔ cup Japanese rice vinegar

⅓ cup sugar

4 teaspoons sea salt

3 inches fresh ginger, peeled, grated, then squeezed in a garlic mincer

3 garlic cloves, crushed

Makes enough rice for 2 sushi rolls, 6 slices each

Wash the rice 5 times in cold water. Let drain in a wire strainer for at least 30 minutes, or overnight.

Put in a saucepan with 2⅓ cups water (the same volume of water plus 15 percent more). Cover tightly and bring to a boil over a high heat. Reduce the heat to medium and boil for 10 minutes. Reduce the heat to low and simmer for 5 minutes. **Do not raise the lid.**

Still covered, let rest for 10 minutes.

Put the vinegar, sugar, salt, ginger, and garlic in a saucepan and heat gently.

Spread the rice over a wide dish, cut through with a rice paddle or wooden spoon, and fan a little to cool. Cut the vinegar mixture through the rice with the spoon.

Use immediately while still tepid. **Do not chill—cold spoils sushi.** (The rice contains vinegar, which will preserve it for a short time.)

The rice is now ready to be assembled in any one of the following ways. For a party, prepare at least 3 kinds, with one of each kind per person.

Variation: Add 1 sheet of kombu seaweed, wiped with a cloth, then slashed several times with a knife, to the rice cooking water. Bring slowly to a boil, then discard the seaweed just before the water reaches boiling point.

Cucumber Sushi

This simple, traditional sushi is a favorite with vegetarians.

1 sheet nori seaweed, toasted

1 quantity sushi rice (see opposite)

½ teaspoon wasabi paste

1 mini cucumber, seeded and sliced lengthwise

Makes 12 Ⓥ

Cut the seaweed in half. Put one piece on a bamboo sushi mat, shiny side down. Divide the rice in 2* and press each portion into a cylinder shape. Put one of the cylinders in the middle of one piece of seaweed and press out the rice to meet the front edge. Press toward the far edge, leaving about ½–1 inch bare.

Brush ¼ teaspoon wasabi down the middle of the rice and put a line of cucumber on top.

Roll the mat gently from the front edge, pinch gently, then complete the roll and squeeze to make a tight cylinder. Make a second cylinder using the remaining ingredients.

The sushi can be wrapped in plastic and left like this until you are ready to cut and serve.

To serve, cut in half with a wet knife and trim off the end (optional—you may like to leave a "cockade" of cucumber sticking out the end). Cut each half in 3 and arrange on a serving platter. Small dishes of Japanese tamari soy sauce, pink pickled ginger, and wasabi paste are traditional accompaniments.

*Note: Sushi rice can be very sticky. To make it easier to handle, the Japanese use "hand vinegar"—a bowl of water with a splash of vinegar added.

73

Sushi Allsorts: Fillings and Toppings

Use your choice of 1–5 of the ingredients listed below and arrange them in a line across the rice 1 inch from the front edge. If using more than 2 fillings, use a whole sheet of seaweed instead of half. The roll is completed and cut as in the main recipe.

- Scallions, finely sliced lengthwise
- Carrots, finely sliced then blanched
- Daikon (mooli), finely sliced lengthwise
- Cucumber, seeded and sliced lengthwise
- Green beans or yard-long beans, blanched
- Red and/or yellow peppers, cored, seeded, and sliced into strips
- Trout or salmon caviar
- Smoked fish, cut into long shreds
- Very fresh fish fillets, sliced and marinated in lime juice or rice vinegar for 30 minutes
- Cooked shrimp, peeled, deveined, and halved lengthwise
- Raw or chargrilled tuna, finely sliced
- Three eggs, beaten, cooked as a very thin omelet, then finely sliced
- Baby spinach leaves, blanched
- Avocado, finely sliced lengthwise

Sushi Accompaniments:

- Soy sauce
- Pink pickled ginger
- Wasabi paste.

Seafood Sushi

2 sheets nori seaweed, toasted

1 quantity cooked sushi rice (page 72)

Toppings such as:
about ¾ cup smoked salmon, salmon, or trout caviar, cooked seafood, or fresh raw fish, such as tuna or salmon

Makes 12

Make 2 sushi rolls as in the previous recipe, using whole sheets of seaweed rather than halves. Do not add filling. When the rolls are made, pat them into rectangular cylinders. Cut each one into 6 and pat into tidy rectangles. Top each one with a spoonful of keta (salmon caviar) or pieces of seafood or fish cut to size.

Sushi Cones

4 sheets nori seaweed, halved (4 x 7 inches) and toasted

2 quantities cooked sushi rice (page 72)

Fillings such as:
enoki mushrooms, raw or smoked salmon, blanched asparagus, finely sliced carrot, cucumber strips, thin omelet, sliced, sesame seeds, wasabi, and pickled ginger

Makes 8

Put a sheet of nori, shiny side down, on a work surface. Put 1 tablespoon rice on the left edge. Using wet hands, spread it lightly to cover one half of the seaweed completely. Add your choice of filling ingredients diagonally across the rice, letting them overlap the top left corner.

To roll the cones, put one finger in the middle of the bottom edge, then roll up the cone from the bottom left, using your finger as the axis of the turn. As each cone is made, put it on a serving platter with the seam down.

74

Stuffed Grape Leaves

I must admit, stuffed grape leaves weren't my favorite thing—until I made my own. If you have vegetarians among your guests, they will adore these leaves. If you're including rice in your stuffing ingredients, make sure it's well seasoned.

36 preserved grape leaves (1–2 packs), plus extra for lining the pan

olive oil, for brushing

1–2 lemons, sliced

boiling vegetable or chicken stock, to cover (see method)

Filling:

1 cup basmati rice

3 tablespoons olive oil

2 onions, finely chopped

3 garlic cloves, crushed

1 cup pine nuts

salt and freshly ground black pepper

2 tablespoons dried mint

½ teaspoon ground allspice

½ teaspoon ground cinnamon

¼ cup finely chopped parsley

3 tomatoes, peeled, seeded, and diced

1 teaspoon sugar

Makes 36 Ⓥ

To make the filling, soak the rice in water to cover for about 30 minutes. Drain.

Heat the oil in a skillet, add the onions and garlic and cook until golden. Add the pine nuts and cook until lightly browned, about 2–3 minutes. Stir in the rice, then add 2 cups water, the salt, pepper, dried mint, allspice, and cinnamon. Stir, bring to a boil, then cover tightly, reduce the heat and simmer gently, without lifting the lid, for 20 minutes.

Remove from the heat—the rice should be perfectly cooked and fluffy. Add the parsley, tomatoes, and sugar. Cool, cover and chill until for up to 2 days.

Soak the grape leaves in cold water for 15 minutes—after 10 minutes, change the water and begin to unfold the leaves, still in the water. Drain. Bring a large saucepan of water to a boil, add the leaves and blanch for 2–3 minutes. Drain, rinse, drain, and pat dry with paper towels.

Put the leaves, shiny side down, on a work surface. Put 1–1½ teaspoons of the filling at the stalk end of the leaf. Fold the stalk end once over the filling, then fold in the 2 sides like an envelope. Roll up, loosely, into a cylinder, finishing with the seam underneath. Pat into an even shape.

Put a layer of leaves over the base of a large, heavy-bottom saucepan. Add the stuffed grape leaves, packing them closely together. Add a layer of lemon slices, then another layer of leaves. Put a heatproof plate on top. Cover with boiling stock, add salt to taste and bring to a boil. Cover, reduce the heat, and simmer for 35 minutes. Let stand, covered, for another 10 minutes, then let cool and brush with olive oil. Serve warm or cool, but not cold.

Though it's not traditional to serve them with a dip, I like them with a spicy Middle-Eastern sauce or hummus sprinkled with chili and parsley.

Variation: The lamb and pine nut filling on page 117 is equally delicious.

Belgian endive and mini lettuce **leaves** make perfect bite-sized edible spoons.

Thai Crab Salad in Endive Leaves

2 red chilies, cored, seeded and finely chopped

1 garlic clove, minced

2 inches lemongrass, very finely chopped

grated zest and juice of 1 lime

1 tablespoon fish sauce

½ cup canned coconut milk

1 teaspoon sugar

1 small onion or shallot, finely chopped, or 2 scallions, finely sliced

salt, to taste

3½ cups cooked crabmeat or shelled, deveined shrimp, finely chopped

1 bunch basil, preferably Asian basil, torn

1 bunch cilantro leaves, torn, plus extra to serve

Belgian endive leaves, preferably red, or mini Little Gem lettuce leaves, to serve

Makes about 24 filled leaves

Put 1 chopped chili, the garlic, lemongrass, lime zest and juice, fish sauce, coconut milk, and sugar in a bowl and mix well until the sugar dissolves. Stir in the onion, shallot, or scallion. Taste and adjust the seasoning.

Fold in the crabmeat or chopped shrimp and herbs, then pile about 1 tablespoon in the base of each endive leaf or lettuce leaf. Serve topped with finely chopped chili and torn cilantro leaves.

Hummus Salad in Crisp Leaves

1 quantity homemade or store-bought hummus

4 mini cucumbers or 1 large cucumber, halved, seeded, and finely diced

3 ripe red tomatoes, seeded and finely diced

1 red Spanish onion, finely chopped

3 tablespoons chopped fresh mint leaves

3 tablespoons fresh cilantro leaves

To serve:

24 Belgian endive or lettuce leaves

sprigs of cilantro

grated zest of 1–2 lemons

Makes about 24 leaves Ⓥ

Put the hummus in a bowl, then fold in the cucumber, tomatoes, onion, mint, and cilantro leaves.

Put 1 tablespoon in each endive or lettuce leaf, arrange on a platter and serve, topped with a sprig of cilantro and grated lemon zest.

Quick, easy, and delicious finger food containers, **leaves** can be filled with one of the recipes in this section, others from this book—or use one of your own favorite mixtures. Any good gourmet store will provide lots of other delicious possibilities. Listed here are just a few serving ideas.

80

Leaf Scoop Fillings:

Your choice of:

- Smoked chicken with Mexican Salsa (page 36), shown this page.

- Shredded turkey and cranberry sauce with cress, shown this page.

- Baba Ganoush eggplant purée (page 36) sprinkled with chopped parsley and toasted sesame seeds, shown opposite. Ⓥ

- Soft goat cheese rolled into balls with a spoonful of salmon or trout caviar, plus pepper and lemon zest, shown opposite.

- Chili Pork Balls (page 102) with Satay Sauce (page 36).

- Soft goat cheese mixed with chopped herbs. Ⓥ

- Smoked salmon and crème fraîche.

- Onion and garlic sautéed in butter or olive oil until almost melted, then mixed with ricotta. Ⓥ

- Felafel (page 106) on a bed of hummus with harissa and mint. Ⓥ

- Quail eggs or small hen eggs, halved, on a spoonful of aioli (page 36) sprinkled with poppy seeds. Ⓥ

- Bocconcini cheeses, halved and topped with red pesto. Ⓥ

- Frikadelle (page 100) with horseradish/wasabi mayonnaise (page 84) and chopped tomato.

- Finely sliced rare roast beef with wasabi mayonnaise (page 84).

- Shredded chicken with sweet spicy mango chutney.

- Vietnamese Mini Spring Rolls (page 112) with *Nuóc Cham* (page 37).

Convenient containers for party food, **wraps and pockets** can be used with specially cooked fillings, store-bought goodies, or other recipes in this book.

Ciabatta Pockets with Rare Roast Beef, Wasabi Mayonnaise and Baby Salad

These pockets are crisp and delicious. Use ciabatta rolls, halved, or the ends of loaves (use the middles to make bruschetta). Other fillings can also be used, such as the Frikadelle or Chili Pork Balls on pages 100–103.

2 lb. beef fillet, in the piece

2 tablespoons olive oil

12 ciabatta rolls, halved

butter, for spreading (optional)

baby salad leaf mixture

sea salt and freshly ground black pepper

Wasabi mayonnaise:

1 egg

1 egg yolk

1 garlic clove, crushed

1 tablespoon lemon juice

sea salt

peanut or sunflower oil (see method)

1 tablespoon wasabi paste or freshly grated horseradish

Makes 24

To roast the beef, heat a heavy-bottom ovenproof skillet or roasting pan on top of the stove, then add the olive oil and swirl to coat the surface.

Add the whole fillet of beef and fry at a high heat on all sides until well browned—about 5 minutes. Remove from the heat. You can prepare the beef in advance to this point.

Preheat the oven to its highest temperature, but at least 400°F. Put the beef, still in its skillet or pan, into the oven and roast 15–20 minutes. Remove from the oven and set aside to set the juices and to let cool.

Cut the beef crossways into ⅛-inch slices, then into strips suitable for stuffing the rolls. (Thicker slices taste better, don't be skimpy!) Cover with plastic.

To make the wasabi mayonnaise, put the egg, egg yolk, garlic, lemon juice, and salt in a small blender or food processor and blend until pale. Add the oil, drop by drop at first, then faster, in stages, to form a thick emulsion. If the mixture becomes too thick, add a tablespoon of warm water. Add the wasabi paste or horseradish and pulse to mix.

Cut the ciabatta rolls in half and make a pocket in each half by pressing with your fingers. Add a smear of butter, if using. Put a pinch of salad leaves in the pocket, 1–2 strips of roast beef, then top with a teaspoon of wasabi mayonnaise.

Variations:
• This combination is also good as a topping for Danish Open Sandwiches (page 46).
• Instead of making your own mayonnaise, use best-quality mayonnaise from a French-style gourmet store. Do not use bottled mayo—better to choose another dressing altogether!

Variation:

Tea-Smoked Chinese Duck

Rub 4 duck breasts with chili oil and 5-spice powder. Chargrill on a stove-top grill-pan, skin-side down, over high heat, until the skin is crispy, about 3 minutes. Remove to a plate.

Put a double layer of foil in a wok, overlapping the edges. Add ½ cup Chinese tea leaves, 2 tablespoons all-purpose flour, 4–6 whole star anise, 1 tablespoon brown sugar and a curl of fresh orange peel or 6 pieces dried tangerine peel. Put a round smoking rack or cake rack on top, then the duck, skin-side up, on top of that. Cover with more foil, then cover tightly with a lid.

Heat the wok until the smoke rises. Smoke for about 10–15 minutes.

Remove the duck and serve immediately or let cool to room temperature.

When ready to serve, finely slice crossways and serve as in the main recipe with salad leaves and a teaspoon of Chinese sauce such as plum or hoisin.

Note: Tea-smoking is also wonderful for fish such as salmon.

Indian Samosas

Freshly cooked and utterly delicious, vegetarian samosas are sold at roadside stalls and railway stations all over India and Pakistan. A great hit at fashionable parties in Bombay and Delhi, these smaller versions are made with phyllo rather than traditional pastry, and rolled into triangles rather than cones. Samosas are usually deep-fried, but can also be oven-baked.

2 potatoes, finely diced

1 carrot, finely diced

1 cup peanut oil

1 small onion, chopped

¼ teaspoon nigella (onion seeds) (optional)

1 cup corn kernels, fresh or frozen

¼ cup shelled peas

4 oz. paneer* or mozzarella cheese

1 tablespoon chopped cilantro

2 red chilies, cored, seeded, and chopped

a pinch of chili powder (optional)

1 teaspoon amchoor (mango powder) or lime juice

½ teaspoon salt

15 sheets ready-made phyllo pastry

melted butter, for brushing

Makes 30 Ⓥ

*Note: Paneer is sold in some large supermarkets and Asian stores. To make your own, see recipe on page 24.

To make the filling, cook the potatoes and carrots in boiling salted water until just cooked, about 3–5 minutes. Drain.

Heat 3 tablespoons of the oil in a wok or saucepan and stir-fry the onion and nigella until the onions are softened and translucent. Add the potatoes, carrot, corn and peas and stir-fry for 1 minute.

Stir in the cheese, cilantro, chilies, chili powder, if using, amchoor or lime juice, and salt. Let cool.

Unwrap the phyllo pastry and put 1 sheet on a work surface. Keep the rest covered with a damp cloth while you work. Cut the sheet of pastry in half and brush the sheets all over with melted butter, fold each half into 3, lengthwise, buttering between, making 2 long strips.

Put 1 tablespoon filling at one corner of pastry. Fold the corner over to form a triangle. Continue folding until the filling is enclosed and the whole strip of pastry has been used. Repeat until all the pastry and filling have been used.

When all the samosas are made, heat the remaining oil to 375°F in a wok or saucepan. Add 2–3 samosas at a time and fry until golden, turning them once.

As each one is cooked, remove and drain on crumpled paper towels, then serve hot, warm or cool.

Variation:
To bake the samosas, put them, spaced apart, on a lightly greased baking tray, brush with a mixture of peanut oil and melted butter. Bake in a preheated oven at 350°F for 15 minutes until crisp and golden.

To Prepare Ahead:
• Cook the day before, cool and chill. Reheat at 350°F for about 10 minutes just before serving.

Empanaditas

India has samosas, England has Cornish pasties, Australia has the meat pie—but Mexico and South America have one of the most delicious of all pastry parcels, the empanada. Empanaditas, the little ones, are perfect as finger food for a party. They are usually made with corn tortilla dough and deep-fried, but to save time, you might like to use ready-rolled puff pastry, then cook them in the oven, as shown in the photograph.

2 cups lean ground beef

1 onion, finely chopped

1 garlic clove, minced

1 tablespoon finely chopped parsley

salt and freshly ground black pepper

1 cup tomato purée

⅓ cup raisins, soaked in water

¼ cup slivered almonds, toasted

⅓ cup dry sherry

1 lb. puff pastry, either fresh ready-made or frozen and thawed

paprika or mild chili powder, for dusting (optional)

Mexican Salsa or Chili Mojo (page 37), to serve

Makes about 40

Heat a non-stick skillet, add the meat and sauté, stirring from time to time, for about 30 minutes, or until browned. Add the onion and garlic, stir-fry for 2 minutes, then add the parsley, salt, pepper, tomato purée, raisins and almonds. Stir-fry until the mixture thickens. Remove from the heat and stir in the sherry. Set aside to develop the flavors.

Roll out the puff pastry to about ⅛-inch thick, then cut out rounds using an 3-inch cookie cutter. Re-roll and cut the trimmings.

Put 1 tablespoon of filling in each circle, slightly off-center. Fold the pastry in half and press the edges with a fork to seal. Chill for 30 minutes.

Arrange apart on baking trays and cook in a preheated oven at 375°F for 15–20 minutes until browned.

Sprinkle with paprika or mild chili powder if using, then serve with a Mexican Salsa or Chili Mojo.

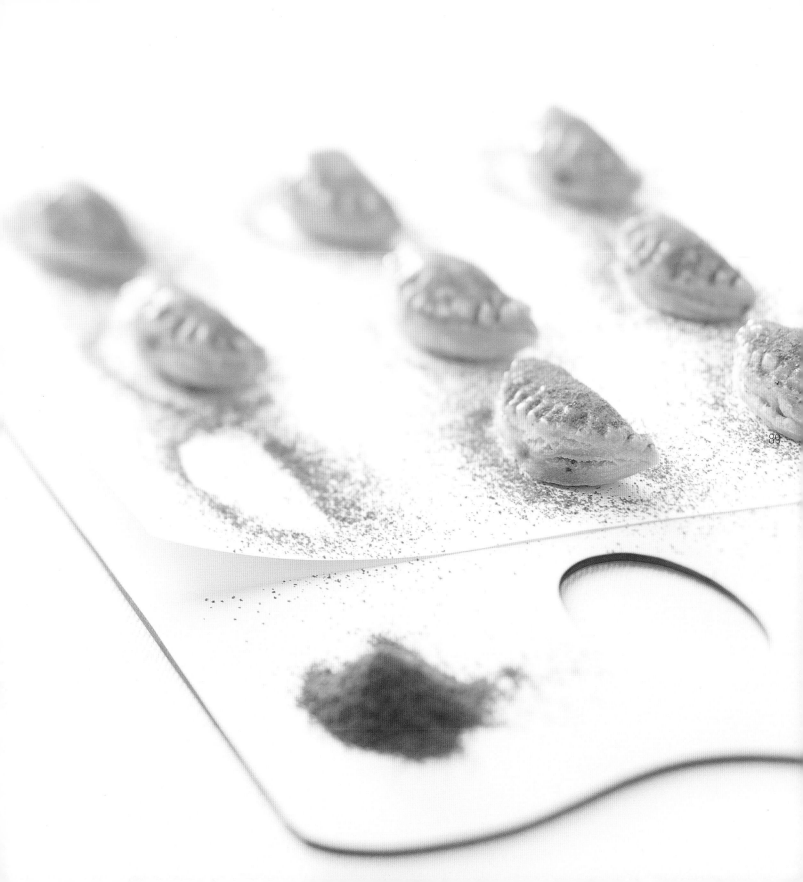

Fresh Vietnamese
Spring Rolls

Vietnamese food is full of flavor
and not as oily as Chinese.
These fresh spring rolls are
delicious. They can be made
several hours in advance; spray
them with a mist of water and
cover with plastic wrap to
prevent them from drying out.
Children love to make them, so
enlist their help.

24 small Vietnamese ricepaper wrappers
(6 inches)*

1 oz. cellophane noodles (1 small bundle),
soaked in boiling water for 20 minutes,
drained, then snipped into 2-inch lengths

3 carrots, finely sliced into matchstick
strips, preferably on a mandoline

1 mini cucumber, halved, seeded, and
finely sliced into matchstick strips

6 scallions, halved then finely sliced
lengthwise

2 baskets enoki mushrooms

fresh mint leaves

fresh cilantro leaves

1 small package fresh bean sprouts,
trimmed, rinsed, and dried

2 cups cooked crabmeat, peeled,
chopped shrimp or stir-fried ground pork

Nuóc Cham dipping sauce, to serve
(page 37)

Makes 24

Assemble all the ingredients on platters
and fill a wide bowl with hot water. Work
on one roll at a time.

Dip 1 ricepaper sheet in the water for
about 30 seconds until softened. Put on
a plate (not a board, which will dry out
the ricepaper).

Put a small pinch of each ingredient in a
line down the middle of the sheet, fold
over both sides of the sheet, then roll up
like a cigar. (If folding only one side, as
shown, let some of the ingredients
protrude from the other end.)

Spray with a mist of water and set aside
on a plate, covered with a damp cloth,
while you prepare the others.

To serve, spray with water again and
serve with the dipping sauce—it's better
to serve a small quantity at a time, in
case they dry out.

*If preferred, stir 1 tablespoon sesame oil
through the noodles after soaking*

*Note: The wrappers come in packs of
50 large or 100 small. Wrap leftover
wrappers in 2 layers of plastic and seal
well. Leftover filling can made into balls or
patties, pan-fried and served with
toothpicks.*

Mini Tortilla Wraps

Tortilla wraps can be made with any number of different filling combinations—just serve your favorites. For a party, however, it's always a good idea to include something for vegetarians—I like avocado.

2 large mild chilies, cored, seeded and halved lengthwise

4 cooked chicken breasts

2 roasted yellow peppers, sliced

20 small flour tortillas

4 Oven-Dried Tomatoes (page 31)

1 romaine lettuce, finely sliced

1 cup Monterey Jack or queso fresco

leaves from 1 large bunch cilantro, torn

lime juice, to sprinkle

salt and freshly ground black pepper

Makes 40

Pan-toast or chargrill the chilies until the skin is blistered. Scrape off the skin, then finely slice the chilies.

Pull the chicken breasts apart into long shreds.

Warm the tortillas, one by one, under the broiler for about 1 minute until they soften and puff slightly.

Place on a work surface and add a layer of each ingredient in a line about ¼–⅓ from the edge of the tortilla. Sprinkle with lime juice, salt, and pepper. Fold over the bottom edge, and one side edge, then roll up into a cylinder. Cut in half crosswise, then serve, seam-side down, or tied in a napkin.

Chicken Souvlaki

All the components for this delicious wrap can be assembled in advance, then wrapped and cut just before serving. Roast lamb can be used instead of the chicken if you like. Make sure the chicken or lamb and breads are warm before assembling—and wrap them up in napkins if you like.

4 chicken breasts, skinned and boned, or lamb leg chops, cut into 1-inch steaks across the bone

salt

Marinade:

4 garlic cloves, crushed

1 tablespoon fresh lemon juice

1 teaspoon cumin seeds, toasted in a dry skillet, then crushed with a mortar and pestle

1 teaspoon freshly ground black pepper

2 tablespoons extra-virgin olive oil

To serve:

1 package soft Middle Eastern flatbread, such as lavash, village bread, or pita

1 cup hummus

1 cup tabbouleh salad, store-bought or homemade*

hot pepper sauce (optional)

6 scallions, cut into strips lengthwise, then blanched in boiling water

Serves about 24

Trim the chicken or lamb. Mix the marinade ingredients together in a shallow non-metal dish, then add the chicken or lamb and turn until well covered. Chill for 20 minutes or overnight to develop the flavors.

To cook the chicken, brush a heavy-bottom skillet with oil, add the drained chicken breasts and sauté gently on each side until tender, about 15 minutes. To cook the lamb, add the steaks to the skillet and cook at a high heat for about 10 minutes on each side until crispy outside and pink inside. Remove from the heat, let rest for 10 minutes, then cut into ⅛-inch strips. Sprinkle with salt, cover and set aside until ready to assemble (reheat if necessary).

To assemble, cut the flatbread into pieces about 4 inches square. Heat the pieces briefly, then put a heaped teaspoon of hummus in the middle, add 1 tablespoon tabbouleh, some sliced chicken or lamb, and a dab of hot pepper sauce, if using. Roll up the bread into a square parcel, folding over each end to enclose the filling. Tie up with the strips of scallion.

*To make your own tabbouleh, soak ½ cup toasted buckwheat in water for 20 minutes, then drain. Skin, deseed, and chop 2 large ripe tomatoes. Chop a large bunch of parsley and another of mint. Finely chop 3 scallions. Put all of the ingredients in a bowl, then toss with 2 tablespoons olive oil, 1 tablespoon lemon juice, a pinch of salt, and lots of freshly cracked black pepper. Taste and adjust the seasoning.

Mini Pita Pockets

Although pita breads are from the Middle East, the nicest I ever had were in Pakistan—delicious mini half-moons filled with crusty roast lamb, mild red onion rings and tahini sauce. Make these with other kinds of fillings such as chicken, duck, or Indian Cheese (page 24), or the Afghan Lamb Kabobs (page 122).

24 mini pita breads, or 12 medium ones, halved

tabbouleh (page 94), salad, or parsley sprigs

24 small slices of roasted lamb or chicken, 24 felafel (page 106) or 24 cubes of cheese, such as paneer or feta

2–3 red onions, finely sliced

about 2 cups tahini sauce or hummus

hot pepper sauce, to taste (optional)

Serves 24

Gently warm the pita breads and cut in half crosswise if large.

Split them open and add a spoonful of tabbouleh, salad, or parsley, a few shreds of roast lamb, chicken, felafel or cheese, a few onion rings, a spoonful of tahini sauce or hummus, and a drop of hot pepper sauce, if using.

Serve stacked in baskets or folded in tiny cocktail napkins.

A collection of delicious **bites and balls** from around the world. Serve them with toothpicks and a dipping sauce—or in pocket breads, on toast, in endive or lettuce leaves, or wrapped in tortillas.

Frikadelle

These delicious meatballs are a traditional dish in Scandinavia, Holland and Germany. Our family recipe includes a seasoning of salted anchovies, which acts a little like fish sauce in Southeast Asian cooking—as a seasoning, rather than a flavoring.

⅓ cup mashed potato

1 cup, firmly packed, ground beef*

½ cup ground veal*

½ cup ground lamb*

½ cup dried breadcrumbs

6 tablespoons light cream

1 egg, beaten

a pinch of freshly grated nutmeg

1 canned anchovy fillet, mashed

a pinch of ground allspice

salt and freshly ground black pepper

3 tablespoons butter

1 small onion, finely chopped

2 tablespoons vegetable oil

rosemary sprigs, for serving

Makes about 30

*Note: The traditional meat combination is
1 cup each of ground pork and veal.

Put the potato in a bowl with the meat, breadcrumbs, cream, egg, nutmeg, anchovy, allspice, a large pinch of salt, and a good grinding of black pepper. Mix well.

Heat 1 tablespoon of the butter in a skillet, add the onion and sauté until softened and translucent. Stir into the meat mixture.

Wet your hands, take 1 tablespoon of the mixture, roll it between your palms to form a ball, then flatten it slightly. Repeat until all the mixture has been used. Arrange the balls apart on a tray, cover with plastic wrap and chill for about 1 hour.

Heat the remaining butter and the oil in a heavy-bottom skillet, then sauté the meatballs, spaced apart, in batches, until browned on both sides. Shake them from time to time. Remove and drain on crumpled paper towels.

Serve with toothpicks or rosemary sprigs—the rosemary gives wonderful fragrance to the frikadelle.

Alternatively, serve with a Chili Dipping Sauce (page 102), or in Hamburger Buns (page 50–53), in pita breads (page 96), as Souvlaki (page 94), in tortilla wraps (page 92), or in ciabatta pockets (page 84) with your choice of salad leaves and sauce.

Vietnamese Pork Balls with Chili Dipping Sauce

A delicious traditional recipe that's perfect for a cocktail party. The original is manna from heaven to the dedicated chili-head. I am not, and find this amount is plenty. Don't just up the chili because you love it—remember some people don't. And of course they'll drink more to cool the fires, never realizing that water or alcohol won't help soothe a chili burn (only milk or yogurt will, in case you're interested!). Use fat Fresno chilies for a mild flavor, or tiny bird's eye chilies for blinding heat.
Fish sauce is used as a seasoning in Vietnamese cooking—like salt or soy sauce. If you can't find it, use salt instead (not as interesting, but OK in a pinch.)

102

Chili dipping sauce:

½ cup white rice vinegar

2–6 small or 1 large red chili, finely sliced

1 tablespoon fish sauce

1 scallion, finely sliced (optional)

½–1 tablespoon brown sugar

Pork balls:

2 cups ground pork

6 garlic cloves, crushed

2 stalks lemongrass, finely sliced

1 bunch cilantro, finely chopped

2 fresh red chilies, cored and diced

1 tablespoon brown sugar

1 tablespoon fish sauce, such as *nam pla*

1 egg, beaten

salt and freshly ground black pepper

peanut oil, for frying

Makes about 12

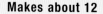

Mix all the ingredients for the chili dipping sauce in a small bowl, stir to dissolve the sugar, then set aside to develop the flavors.

To make the pork balls, put all the remaining ingredients except the peanut oil in a bowl and mix well. Dip your hands in water, take about 1–2 tablespoons of the mixture, and roll it into a ball. Repeat with the remaining mixture. Put the balls, spaced apart, on a plate as you finish them. Chill for at least 30 minutes.

Fill a wok one-third full of peanut oil and heat to 375°F or until a cube of bread browns in 30 seconds. Add the pork balls, 6 at a time, and deep-fry in batches until golden brown. Remove and drain on crumpled paper towels, keeping them warm in the oven until all the balls are done. Serve with the chili dipping sauce.

Thai Crabcakes with Chili Dipping Sauce

104

Everyone loves Thai fishcakes and crabcakes. Chopped green beans or chopped asparagus are popular with western chefs, but I prefer snake beans (Chinese long beans)—they have better texture and a more interesting taste.

3 red chilies, cored

3 scallions, finely sliced

2 garlic cloves, crushed

4 cilantro stalks, finely chopped

1 inch fresh ginger or galangal, chopped

6 kaffir lime leaves, finely sliced, or grated zest of 2 limes

1 tablespoon fish sauce

8 oz. boneless fish fillets, such as cod

1½ cups crabmeat (fresh, frozen, or canned)

2 Chinese long beans or 12 beans, finely sliced

1 oz. beanthread (cellophane) noodles (1 small bundle)

1 egg, beaten

2 tablespoons peanut oil, for frying

Chili dipping sauce:

½ cup white rice vinegar or lime juice

1 red chili, finely sliced

1 tablespoon fish sauce, such as *nam pla*

1 scallion, finely sliced

1 teaspoon brown sugar

Makes about 30

Put the chilies, scallions, garlic, cilantro stalks, ginger or galangal, kaffir lime leaves or lime zest, and fish sauce in a food processor and work to a paste. Add the fish and work to a paste. Transfer to a bowl and mix in the crabmeat and beans.

Soak the beanthread noodles in a bowl of hot water for 5 minutes, then drain and snip into short pieces, about 1 inch long. Mix into the fish and stir in the beaten egg. Wet your hands with water and shape the mixture into flat hamburger-shaped patties of 1–2 tablespoons each.

Heat the oil in a wok or skillet and swirl to coat the sides. Add the crabcakes, 3 at a time, and sauté until golden. Transfer to a plate lined with crumpled paper towels and keep them hot in the oven while you cook the remaining crabcakes.*

Mix the dipping sauce ingredients together in a small bowl and serve with the crabcakes.

*Note: The crabcakes can also be deep-fried in a wok about one-third full of oil. The patties can also be sprinkled with rice flour before cooking.

Felafel

This popular Middle Eastern recipe is traditionally made with dried, soaked chickpeas. Some western recipes substitute canned and drained chickpeas, but this will produce very soft felafel, probably too delicate to serve as fingerfood. Felafel are perfect for vegetarian guests—if the carnivores don't eat them all first.

1 cup dried chickpeas or 2 cups canned chickpeas, drained

1 cup dried fava beans or 2 cups frozen fava beans

1 large bunch parsley sprigs, chopped

3 tablespoons chopped fresh mint leaves

½ cup bulgar wheat, soaked in hot water to cover for 15 minutes

4 garlic cloves, minced

1 egg

1 teaspoon ground cumin (optional)

1 teaspoon cardamom seeds, freshly crushed, or 1 teaspoon ground coriander

½ teaspoon baking soda

salt and freshly ground black pepper

3 scallions, chopped

1 leek, white only, or 1 onion chopped

1 red pepper, seeded and chopped

about ¼ cup sesame seeds

peanut, corn, or sunflower oil, for frying

sprigs of cilantro, to serve

Makes about 20 Ⓥ

Soak the dried chickpeas and fava beans overnight in water to cover. Drain.

If using frozen fava beans, let thaw, rinse in cold water, and drain.

Put the chickpeas and fava beans into a food processor. Add the parsley, mint, bulgar wheat, garlic, egg, ground cumin, cardamom or coriander, baking soda, salt, and pepper. Pulse until coarsely blended. Transfer to a bowl.

Put the scallions, leek or onion, and red pepper in the food processor and pulse briefly until very finely chopped. Tip the bean mixture back into the food processor and pulse to mix. (Work in batches if necessary).

Set aside for 15 minutes, then chill for 30 minutes.

Moisten your hands and pinch off pieces of bean mixture about 1-inch diameter. Shape into balls with your hands. Spread the sesame seeds on a small plate or saucer and roll half the balls in the seeds pressing them into the surface. Leave the other half plain.

Pour 1¼-inch depth of oil into a large skillet or wok. Heat to 370°F or until a cube of bread browns in 30 seconds. Cook in batches until brown, about 2 minutes, turning after 1 minute.

Drain on crumpled paper towels, then serve topped with sprigs of cilantro.

Serving Variations:
• *Serve with wooden toothpicks and a dip from pages 36–37.*
• *Serve in halved mini pita breads (page 97) with salad and hummus.*
• *Serve in mini lettuce leaves with a spoonful of hummus and a sprig of mint (pages 80–81).*

107

Delicious, bite-sized morsels, **wontons and satays** make perfect finger food, and many can be prepared ahead of time.

Chinese Purses

This is wonderful party food, adapted from a recipe on loan from a food-writing friend who gives wonderful parties. Get 4 large bamboo steamers from Chinatown (they aren't expensive) and 2 lids. You can serve one set of 2 while the next set is cooking. If you leave a space in the middle of the steaming rack to put the bowl of dipping sauce, you can cook and serve in the same bamboo container. This can look very stylish, especially if you use banana leaves to line the rack (paper or cabbage leaves will do just as well, but banana leaves give a very delicate extra flavor).

110

1¾ cups ground pork or chicken

⅓ cup shelled shrimp (optional)

2 slices bacon, chopped

1 teaspoon crushed Szechuan pepper or freshly ground black pepper

1 egg white

1 teaspoon sesame oil

2 garlic cloves, crushed

1 inch fresh ginger, grated

a pinch of salt

6 scallions, white and green parts, finely sliced

4 canned water chestnuts, finely diced

4 Chinese long beans or 12 green beans, finely sliced

2 packages small (4-inch) wonton wrappers*

dipping sauce such as soy sauce, chili sauce, or *Nuóc Cham* (page 37), to serve

Makes about 40

Packages vary, but usually contain about 40 large (5-inch) or 70 small (4-inch) wrappers. Leftover wrappers can be frozen.

Put the pork or chicken, shrimp, if using, and bacon into a food processor and blend to a purée. Add the pepper, egg white, sesame oil, garlic, ginger, salt and blend again.

Put all the remaining ingredients except the wonton wrappers and dipping sauce in a bowl, add the meat mixture and mix well. Cover and chill while you prepare the wrappers.

Using a cookie cutter or scissors, cut the wrappers into circles.

Put 1 tablespoon of the filling in the middle of each circle and spread the mixture almost to the edges. Put the circle on the palm of your hand and cup your hand, pressing down the filling with a spatula: you will achieve an open purse with a pleated top. Tap the base gently on the work surface to make a flat bottom, then neaten the pleated tops with your fingers. Repeat until all the purses are made.

Line several layers of a steamer, preferably bamboo, with banana leaves or parchment paper. Put the steamers, in tiers if preferred, into a wok, pour in boiling water to come just below the base of the steamer, cover and steam until done, about 7–10 minutes. Add extra boiling water as necessary.

Serve the purses, still in the steaming racks, with one or more small dishes of dipping sauce. Put the next batch of steamers on to cook while you serve the first batch of purses.

Vietnamese Mini Spring Rolls

These easy-to-make Vietnamese spring rolls are fresher and less oily than Chinese, even though fried. Remember, don't include fried items in your party if your kitchen is close to or part of the party area. The smells of frying are not conducive to attractive party-giving.

You can make the spring rolls in advance, then freeze and fry them from frozen—or fry in advance, then reheat in the oven before serving.

1 oz. cellophane noodles (1 small bundle)

5 Chinese dried cloud ear mushrooms or fresh button mushrooms, finely diced

½ cup ground pork

½ onion, finely chopped

3 garlic cloves, crushed

3 scallions, finely sliced

¼ cup crabmeat (fresh, frozen, or canned and drained) or finely chopped shrimp

salt and freshly ground black pepper

1 package large Vietnamese ricepaper wrappers (50 sheets)*

peanut or corn oil, for frying

To serve (optional):

mini lettuce leaves, such as Little Gem

grated carrot

sprigs of basil

sprigs of cilantro

Nuóc Cham dipping sauce (page 37)

Makes about 40 mini rolls

The wrappers come in packs of 50 large or 100 small. Wrap leftover wrappers in 2 layers of plastic and seal well. Leftover filling can be made into balls or patties, shallow-fried and served with toothpicks.

Soak the noodles in hot water for 20 minutes. Drain and snip into short lengths. Soak the dried mushrooms in boiling water to cover for 30 minutes, then drain and chop. Put the noodles, mushrooms, pork, onion, garlic, scallions, crabmeat, salt, and pepper in a food processor and pulse to mix.

Put 4 ricepapers in a bowl of warm water and let soften for 1–2 minutes. Cut each one into 4 segments. Put 1 segment on a work surface, put 1 teaspoon of filling next to the curved edge and pat the filling into a small cylinder. Fold the curved edge over the filling, fold over the 2 sides like an envelope, then roll up towards the long pointed end. Press to seal. Repeat with all the other wrappers.

Fill a wok one-third full of peanut or corn oil and heat to 375°F or until a piece of noodle fluffs up immediately. Put 5–6 spring rolls into the oil and fry until crisp and golden. Remove and drain on crumpled paper towels. Repeat until all the spring rolls are cooked.

Serve plain, or in baby lettuce leaves with grated carrot, basil, and cilantro sprigs. *Nuóc Cham* (page 36) is the traditional dipping sauce.

Variation: Try the fresh, uncooked Spring Rolls on page 90.

Crispy Pork Wontons

These crispy crunchy wontons produce lots of pizzazz for very little effort. Try this pork filling, or substitute other meats such as chicken, or seafood like crab or chopped shrimp. Wonton wrappers are enormously versatile. They come in packs of 40 large 5-inch or 70 small 4-inch wrappers and are found in the chilled food section of Chinese supermarkets. They should be used within 1–2 days of purchase, but can be frozen if you need to keep them longer.

1 cup ground pork

4 garlic cloves, minced

4 water chestnuts, chopped

4 scallions, white and green parts halved lengthwise, then sliced crosswise

salt and freshly ground black pepper

1 package small wonton wrappers

1 egg, beaten with a drop of water

peanut or sunflower oil

Makes about 40

Put the pork in a bowl with the garlic, water chestnuts, scallions, salt, and pepper and mix well, using your hands or a spoon.

Take the wonton wrappers out of the plastic bag, but keep them covered with a damp cloth or the plastic as you work, because they can dry out quickly.

Put 1 wrapper on the work surface and put about ½ tablespoon of filling in the middle. Brush a circle of beaten egg around the filling. Pull up the sides of the wrapper and twirl or press it together to form a "waist." Open out the top of the wrapper to form a frill. Repeat until all the wontons are made.

Fill a wok one-third full of peanut or sunflower oil and heat to 375°F. To test, drop in a fragment of wonton wrapper—it should fluff up immediately when the oil is the right temperature.

Working in batches, add the wontons 3–4 at a time and fry for a few minutes on each side until brown and crisp. Don't let the oil get too hot, or the dough will cook before the filling.

As each batch is complete, transfer to a plate covered with crumpled paper towels (skim debris off the oil between batches).

Serve hot, with a dipping sauce from page 37 or plain soy sauce.

- *The wontons can be deep-fried, then cooled and frozen. Reheat from frozen for 15 minutes in a preheated oven at 300°F before serving.*
- *The wontons can be assembled and frozen before cooking, but if so, make sure the meat has never been frozen before.*
- *They can also be cooked early in the day of the party, then cooled quickly and refrigerated until ready to serve. Reheat for about 10 minutes in a preheated oven at 400°F.*

114

Middle Eastern Lamb Boats

The filling for these delicious little morsels should be well seasoned, before and after cooking.

1 tablespoon peanut oil or corn oil, plus extra for greasing

1 package pine nuts, about 3–4 oz.

1 cup ground lamb or beef

1 onion, grated

1 garlic clove, minced

¼ cup chopped fresh parsley

1 lb. ready-made shortcrust pastry dough

1 egg, beaten with water, to glaze

sea salt and freshly ground black pepper

To serve (optional):

finely chopped fresh parsley

sea salt flakes

several baking trays, greased

Makes 150

Heat the oil in a skillet, add the pine nuts and stir-fry them quickly until golden, about 30 seconds.

Put the meat, onion, garlic, parsley, pine nuts, salt, and pepper in a bowl and mix well. Set aside.

Roll out the dough to about ⅛-inch thick. Using a long ruler and a sharp knife, trim the edges straight, then cut the dough into long strips about 1 inch wide, then across to make squares. Cover the dough while you make up the boats.

Brush egg glaze down two opposite sides of the square, then put about ½ teaspoon of filling in the middle of the square. Fold in half, with the glazed edges together, place on the work surface with the open side upward. Widen the opening to show the filling and make a boat shape, then tap the boat on your work surface to flatten the bottom. Pinch up the prow and stern to force up the filling.

Put the boats close together in a single layer on greased baking trays. Bake in a preheated oven at 350°F for about 45 minutes or until golden brown and still moist.

Serve immediately, sprinkled with parsley and sea salt flakes, if using.

Sticks and skewers

are an efficient way to serve finger food.

Fish, meat, poultry, or vegetables can be threaded onto skewers and served in a number of different ways.

Each country seems to have its own version of this dish and just a few are listed here. They are easy to organize for a party, but try not to overdo the concept.

One version is perfect, two are delicious—but I wouldn't do more than three for one party. Serve them alone, or with one of the dips from the collection on pages 36–37.

Lemongrass Sticks

The chicken mixture can be cooked on other kinds of skewers, but the lemongrass gives delicious flavor. You can buy ready-made Thai curry pastes, but the recipe given here is especially delicious. The lemongrass infuses the meat with delicate fragrance.

1½ lb. boneless chicken pieces

2 tablespoons peanut oil

1 cup desiccated coconut, soaked for 30 minutes in 1 cup boiling water, then drained

1 large red chili, cored, seeded, and finely chopped

2 tablespoons brown sugar

grated zest of 1 lime

sea salt and freshly ground black pepper

10–20 lemongrass stalks, either whole or halved lengthwise, or satay sticks

Spice paste:

12 Thai shallots or 1 regular shallot, sliced

6 garlic cloves, sliced

2 red chilies, cored, seeded, and sliced

1 inch fresh ginger, peeled and chopped

1 teaspoon turmeric powder

2 teaspoons coriander seeds, crushed

1 teaspoon black peppercorns, crushed

6 almonds, crushed

1 tablespoon fish sauce

2 cloves, crushed

Makes about 20

Remove and discard the skin from the chicken, then put the flesh in a food processor and grind to a paste.

Put all the spice paste ingredients into a small blender or spice grinder (coffee mill) and blend to paste. Heat the oil in a small skillet add the paste and sauté for 5 minutes. Cool, then put in a bowl with the chicken, coconut, chopped chilies, sugar, lime zest, salt, and pepper. Mix well.

Take 2 tablespoons of the mixture and mold it onto the end of the lemongrass stalks or satay skewers. Wrap the ends of the stalks in little squares of foil to prevent them from burning.

Cook over a barbecue or under the broiler until cooked and golden, about 5–10 minutes, then serve.

119

Yakitori

Small versions of yakitori, one of the best-known of all Japanese dishes, can be made for a party. Chicken thighs have better flavor and are always used in this dish. You can buy yakitori sauce—the Japanese variety is of course the best—but it's simple to make your own. Some of the ingredients are only sold in the largest supermarkets or in Asian markets. If you can't find them, there are plenty of other treatments listed here. Although green peppers are traditional, personally I prefer red or yellow ones, especially the long pointed Italian ones which are so much easier to peel.

120

10 chicken thighs, bones removed, skin intact, cut into 1-inch cubes (about 3 pieces per thigh)

10 scallions or baby leeks, halved lengthwise, then cut into ½-inch lengths

4 fresh shiitake mushrooms or white mushrooms, cut into ½-inch squares

4 red or yellow bell peppers, cored, seeded, and cut into ½-inch squares

Japanese 7-spice or crushed black pepper

Yakitori sauce:

2 cups soy sauce

1 cup chicken stock

1 cup sake (or vodka)

1 cup mirin (sweetened Chinese rice wine)

½ cup sugar

Makes about 30

To make the sauce, put all the sauce ingredients in a saucepan, bring to a boil and simmer for 15 minutes—the quantity should be reduced by about one-third. Remove from the heat, let cool, then chill until ready to use (no more than 2 days). Pour half the mixture into a small dipping bowl and reserve the remainder.

Thread the chicken and vegetables onto the skewers. For a meal, 5 pieces would be threaded onto each skewer. For finger food, use 1 piece each of chicken, scallion or leek, mushroom, and pepper. Leave a little space between each item on the skewer so they will cook through.

Cook under a very hot broiler, turning frequently, until the juices rise to the surface, then paint with the reserved yakitori sauce and continue cooking, turning and basting until the chicken is done, about 5–10 minutes in all.

Paint once more with the yakitori sauce and serve the skewers on a platter, sprinkled with Japanese 7-spice or black pepper and with the bowl of dipping sauce beside.

Note: I also like yakitori with furikake seasoning—a mixture of toasted sesame seeds, red shiso, and nori seaweed, sold in Japanese shops and larger supermarkets.

Tandoori Chicken

This is the best tandoori chicken you'll ever taste, and probably the most authentic. It was taught to me by Manjit Gill, one of the finest chefs in India, from what is probably the world's best Indian restaurant, the Bokhara in Delhi's Maurya Sheraton Hotel. Tandoori dishes, which originate in the beautiful Northwest Frontier provinces, make perfect finger food and many can be served still on their skewers.

1½ lb. boneless, skinless chicken pieces

butter or oil, for basting

First marination:

2 teaspoons salt

2 inches fresh ginger, peeled and grated

4 garlic cloves, crushed to a paste

2 tablespoons malt or white rice vinegar

Second marination:

3 tablespoons grated Monterey Jack cheese

1 small egg

4 green chilies, seeded and chopped

1 tablespoon chopped fresh cilantro

1 tablespoon cornstarch

½ cup light cream

To serve:

lemon wedges or lime wedges

finely chopped parsley or cilantro

Makes about 20

Cut the chicken into 1-inch cubes. Pat dry. Put the ingredients for the first marination—the salt, ginger, garlic, and vinegar—in a bowl and stir well. Add the chicken cubes, turn to coat and set aside for 15 minutes.

Put all the ingredients for the second marination into a small food processor and pulse until well mixed.

Remove the chicken from the first marinade and squeeze gently to remove excess moisture. Put into a clean bowl and add the second marinade. Turn in the marinade and massage it in with your fingers. Set aside for 30 minutes. Soak about 20 wooden skewers in water for 30 minutes, then drain.

Thread 1 chicken piece onto the end of each skewer. Cook for 5–8 minutes under a hot broiler or in the oven until half-cooked (put a tray on the shelf underneath to collect the drippings). Remove from the oven and set the skewers upright in a bowl for 5 minutes so excess moisture can drain away

Baste with melted butter or oil and return to the broiler or oven until done, about 5–8 minutes more. Remove from the oven or broiler, sprinkle with fresh lemon juice and chopped parsley or cilantro and serve on a platter.

Afghan Lamb Kabobs

All through Pakistan and Afghanistan, roadside barbecuers cook skewers of lamb, chicken, and occasionally beef on long, sword-like skewers. They're much less alarming on wooden skewers. Muslim cooks wouldn't use wine in the marinade, but I think it improves the flavor enormously.

1 small leg of lamb

3 inches fresh ginger, peeled and grated

4 garlic cloves, crushed

½ bottle red wine, or to cover

ghee (clarified butter) or oil, for brushing

salt and freshly ground black pepper

finely chopped parsley and chili, to serve

Makes about 40

Get the butcher to cut the leg of lamb into thick slices across the bone, about 1 inch thick.

Remove and discard the central bone from each slice, then cut the meat into 1-inch cubes. Put in a bowl, add the ginger and garlic and turn until well covered. Add the wine, then marinate in the refrigerator for at least 2 hours or up to 2 days.

Remove from the marinade and pat dry with paper towels. Thread onto soaked bamboo or metal skewers, brush with melted ghee or oil and sprinkle with sea salt and freshly ground black pepper.

Cook on a barbecue or under a very hot broiler for about 5 minutes on each side, until the meat is crisp and brown outside and still pink inside. Serve sprinkled with finely chopped parsley and chili.

Singapore Pork Satays

Chinese food in Singapore is an interesting mixture of traditional Chinese and Southeast Asian influences. Serve these satays with a Chinese-style soy sauce dip, or a Southeast-Asian-influenced sauce made with fish sauce or peanuts.

2 lb. boneless pork loin

1 tablespoon coriander seeds

½ teaspoon ground turmeric

1 teaspoon salt

1 tablespoon brown sugar

1 stalk lemongrass, finely sliced

5 small shallots, finely chopped

½ cup sunflower or peanut oil

1 cucumber, quartered lengthwise, seeded, and sliced crosswise

1 quantity dipping sauce such as soy sauce, Satay Sauce, or *Nuóc Cham* (pages 36–37), to serve

Makes 20

Cut the pork into 1-inch slices, then each slice into 1-inch cubes.

Put the coriander seeds into a dry skillet and heat over a moderate heat until aromatic. Using a mortar and pestle or spice grinder (or clean coffee mill), grind to a powder. Transfer to a shallow bowl, then add the turmeric, salt, and sugar.

Put the finely sliced lemongrass and shallots in a spice grinder or small blender and work to a paste (add a little water if necessary). Add to the bowl and stir well. Stir in a quarter of the oil.

Add the cubes of meat and turn to coat in the mixture. Cover and set aside to marinate in the refrigerator for 2 hours or overnight.

Soak 20 wooden skewers in water for at least 30 minutes, then drain.

Thread 2 pieces of pork onto each soaked wooden skewer and brush with oil. Cool over medium heat on a barbecue or under a broiler until cooked. Thread a piece of cucumber onto the end of each skewer and serve with the sauce.

Indonesian Beef Satays

Satay sauce, made with peanuts, is one of Indonesia's best-known contributions to world cuisine. Make these skewers with other meats, such as chicken or pork—even lamb—and serve with the creamy, spicy sauce.

1 lb. lean beef

½ cup coconut milk

juice of 2 limes (about ⅓ cup)

2 fresh red chilies, finely chopped

3 stalks lemongrass, finely chopped

3 garlic cloves, minced

2 teaspoons ground coriander

1 teaspoon ground cumin

1 teaspoon ground cardamom

2 tablespoons fish sauce or soy sauce

grated kaffir lime zest

1 teaspoon sugar

peanut oil, for brushing

Satay Sauce, to serve (page 36)

Makes about 10

Cut the beef crosswise into thin strips, about ⅛-inch thick and 2 inches long. Mix the coconut milk, lime juice, chilies, lemongrass, garlic, coriander, cumin, cardamom, fish sauce or soy sauce, lime zest, and sugar in a bowl. Add the beef strips and stir to coat. Cover and chill for 2 hours or overnight to develop the flavors.

Soak 10 bamboo skewers in water for at least 30 minutes, then drain.

Drain the beef, discarding the marinade. Thread the beef in a zig-zag pattern onto the soaked skewers and cook under a hot broiler or in a skillet (brushed with a film of peanut oil) until browned and tender. Serve on a platter with a small bowl of Satay Sauce.

To Prepare Ahead:

• *All the satays in this chapter can be assembled the day before cooking.*

Serving **sweet things** will help bring your party to a delicious end—and a party's not a party without lots of wonderful **drinks**. Preferably champagne, of course, but a truly amazing cocktail can't be beaten.

Dry Martini

This is the finest and best of all cocktails, the dryest dry martini. Traditionally served with an olive, I prefer it "Up with a Twist" (no rocks, with a twist of lemon). Many people prefer martinis made with vodka, so offer an alternative if you like.
The classic mixture, by the way, isn't as dry as this—it's one part dry vermouth to three parts gin.

1 measure best-quality gin

1–2 drops of dry vermouth

a curl of lemon zest or an olive on a toothpick

Serves 1

Stir the gin and vermouth together with ice, then strain into martini glasses.

Note: Traditionally, martinis are "stirred not shaken," or at least James Bond says they are. Personally, I wonder what's to bruise! Shake away if you like!

Sweet things

signal the end of the party.

I find I don't drink any more alcohol after eating something sweet. These few ideas are easy and spectacular, but absolutely nothing beats a large bowl of strawberries or truly fabulous chocolates— if you're into making your own chocolate, this is your chance to show off your skills!

Spiced Fresh Fruit

A favorite way of serving fruit in India. You'd never think that salt and chili would make fruit taste good, but both spark up the flavor amazingly.

a selection of very ripe fruit, such as green or orange melons, apples, guavas (preferably pink), and small pineapples

salt

chili powder or crushed chilies

Serves 1–2 pieces each

If using melons, cut crosswise into thirds, then peel and deseed each piece and cut into 1-inch segments.

If using guavas, pink or white, peel if preferred, then cut into 8 wedges. Spear the wedges lengthwise.

If using pineapples, cut into wedges lengthwise, peel and core, then cut into triangular segments and serve in the same way as the melons.

Prepare any other fruits in bite-sized pieces, peeled if necessary.

Spear each piece vertically with a toothpick or bamboo skewer. Sprinkle with a mixture of salt and chili powder or crushed chilies, or offer separately.

Note: Take care if serving fruit such as apples or pears. They turn brown easily, so should be brushed with lemon juice first.

Flavored Gelato

This easy ice cream is good served in mini brioches, but I also like them in spoons or tiny shot glasses (before the advent of wafer cones, ice cream was served in tiny cone-like glasses). Use vanilla (preferably beans) as a flavoring, or one of the alternatives listed on this page.

2 cups milk

2 vanilla beans, split lengthwise or ¼ teaspoon best-quality vanilla extract (optional)

3–4 egg yolks

¾ cup sugar

1 cup heavy cream

Your choice of flavorings such as:

¼ cup Strega or Grand Marnier

1 lb. ripe peaches poached in ¾ cup sugar, plus water to cover, then peeled, pitted, and puréed

1 basket raspberries or blackberries, either puréed and strained, or crushed with a fork

pulp and seeds of 6 ripe passionfruit

1 cup canned mango purée (Indian is best)

6 pieces of stem ginger, finely chopped, and 6 tablespoons syrup from the jar

Makes about 6–8 cups

To make the basic gelato, heat the milk with the vanilla beans or vanilla extract, until just below boiling point. Set aside to infuse for about 15 minutes. Remove the vanilla beans, if using, and scrape out the seeds with the point of a knife. Stir the seeds back into the milk and discard the beans.

Beat the egg yolks until creamy, then beat 2 tablespoons of the hot milk into the egg yolks, then the remaining milk, a little at a time. Add the sugar and stir until dissolved.

Transfer to a double boiler and cook, stirring, over a gentle heat until the mixture coats the back of a spoon. Alternatively, put into a bowl set over a pan of simmering water (the water must not touch the bowl), and cook in the same way. Do not let boil, or the mixture will curdle.

Remove from the heat, dip the pan into cold water to stop the cooking process, then cool and stir in the cream. Divide the gelato mixture into 2–4 parts, add a different flavoring to each portion, then churn each one separately in an ice cream making machine.

Transfer to freezer-proof boxes, cover and keep in the freezer until ready to serve.

Soften in the refrigerator for about 20 minutes before serving.

Note: A simpler mango ice cream can be made by mixing 1 cup canned mango purée (preferably Indian) with 1 cup heavy cream and about 2–4 tablespoons sugar. Stir until the sugar dissolves, then churn. Don't whip the cream first or you'll get little buttery bits in the mixture.

129

Mini Brioches

You may be able to buy mini brioches where you live, but I can't. So this recipe is just in case. Brioche dough is very soft, sticky, and slack, so it is far easier to make and handle if you use an electric mixer with a dough hook attached.
This recipe makes lots of little brioches. If you need less than this for your party, make half or a quarter and use the remaining mixture to make breakfast-sized brioches.

2½ cups unbleached white bread flour, plus extra for dusting

1½ teaspoons salt

¾ cake compressed yeast*

2 tablespoons milk, lukewarm

6 eggs

¾ cup unsalted butter, softened

peanut oil, for greasing the plastic wrap

petit fours paper cases and several baking trays

Makes 84 ⓥ

*If using active dry yeast, mix one ¼ oz. package with the flour and salt. Make a well in the center, add 5 eggs and the milk and proceed with the recipe.

Mix the flour and salt in the bowl of an electric mixer. Make a well in the center.

Crumble the compressed yeast in a small bowl, add the milk and mix until creamy. Lightly beat 5 of the eggs and pour into the well followed by the creamy yeast mixture. Mix to a soft dough, then fit the dough hooks and knead the dough at a low speed until smooth and elastic, about 5–8 minutes. (The dough will be very sticky and slack.)

Cover with lightly greased plastic wrap or a damp cloth. Let rise at room temperature until doubled in size, about 1–1½ hours.

Punch down the risen dough, then add the soft butter, ¼ cup at a time, mixing well before adding more. Continue beating for about 5 minutes until the dough is smooth, elastic, and very glossy.

To shape the brioche, cut off one third of the dough and reserve, covered with greased plastic wrap.

Pull off pieces of dough the size of a large hazelnut and shape into balls. Put into *petit fours* paper cases set on baking trays. For the tops, pinch off pieces of the reserved dough, about the size of a raisin and shape into tiny balls. Make a small indentation in the center of each brioche base and press in the tops. Cover and let rise as before until doubled in size, about 30–45 minutes.

Lightly beat the remaining egg and brush the tops of the brioche to glaze. Bake in a preheated oven at 400°F for about 15 minutes until golden brown. Let cool on a wire rack, then split and fill with gelato just before serving.

• Use immediately or store in an airtight container for up to 3 days.
• Freeze in freezerproof container for up to 1 month.
• Defrost at room temperature for about 15 minutes.
• Reheat in a preheated oven at 350°F for about 5 minutes.

Gelato in brioche

These sweet icy treats are a marvelous finish to a summer party. Buy the gelato if you like, but make sure it's high-quality. In case you want to make your own, I give my favorite recipe on page 129—with lots of flavoring variations. Of course, if you want just the ice cream, you can hand out mini cones, or little tubs with wooden paddle-spoons.

24 mini brioches (see recipe opposite)

about 1 cup gelato or ice cream

Serves 24

Cut a lid off each brioche at an angle, scoop out most of the soft inside and discard or use for another purpose.

Put a heaped spoonful of gelato in the hole and put the lid on top. Serve immediately on a chilled glass plate.

Mini Croissants with Mincemeat and Brandy Cream

Mini croissants are now widely available in supermarkets, especially at Christmas, while croissant dough is available in larger supermarkets year-round. You can stuff these with mincemeat in advance, so all you have to do is reheat them and top with brandy cream just before serving. Delicious.

24 mini croissants, cheese or plain*

1 jar (about 1 lb.) luxury mincemeat

Brandy cream:

1 cup heavy cream

3 tablespoons confectioners' sugar

3 tablespoons brandy or Cognac

Serves 24

To make the Brandy Cream, whip the cream and sugar together, then whip in the brandy or Cognac.

Cut a lengthwise slit in the top of each croissant. Press a teaspoon of mincemeat into the slit. (The dish can be prepared ahead to this point.)

Reheat in a preheated oven at 350°F for 5 minutes. Arrange on a serving platter and top each one with a teaspoon of whipped brandy cream.

*Note: If mini croissants aren't available, you can make your own using the canned ready-to-bake kind—8 oz. makes 6. You open the can and the dough emerges, ready-cut into 6 triangles for you to roll up and bake yourself. Cut each triangle into 4 smaller triangles (cut off the point, then cut the remaining piece into 3), giving 24 small triangles. Roll up from the long edge leaving the point on top. Bake according to the package instructions, usually at 400°F, but for a shorter time, about 10 minutes, until puffed and golden brown.

Mini Christmas Cakes

At Christmas, everyone will have had their fill of Christmas cake. But it's always nice to suggest the season.

1 section of moist Christmas cake, about 8 x 3 x 3 inches deep

1 package fondant icing, about 1 lb.

Makes about 70 pieces Ⓥ

Cut the sides, top and base off the Christmas cake with a very sharp knife, giving smooth edges. Cut the cake into 1-inch strips lengthwise. Cut each strip into 1-inch strips to make square logs.

Roll out the fondant icing to about ⅛-inch thick, then, using a sharp knife and a metal ruler, cut out rectangular strips 8 x 5 inches wide.

Place one cake "log" on one of the strips and wrap the fondant around it. Press to seal, tap each surface onto the work surface to form sharp corners. Cover with plastic and chill in the refrigerator for at least 30 minutes.

Just before serving, cut the "logs" into 1-inch lengths and serve, perhaps with strong espresso coffee.

Mango and Ginger Kir Royale

Kir Royale is cassis with champagne. This party drink is based on that idea, and if you serve it, you won't have to worry about providing anything else. For my mango and ginger version, I use canned Indian Alphonso mango purée when I'm outside mango growing country, and huge ripe Bowen mangoes from Queensland when I'm in Australia. If you're using fresh mangoes, you'll have to add a little lemon juice to develop the flavor, and ice to help smash the fiber.

1 jar stem ginger, pieces cut into quarters

2 cups mango purée

¼ cup ginger purée or juice*

syrup from the jar of stem ginger

sugar (to taste)

6 bottles chilled champagne (8 glasses per bottle for champagne cocktails)

Makes at least 50 glasses

Thread the quarter pieces of ginger, lengthwise, onto the end of a long toothpick or bamboo skewer. Arrange them on a plate, ginger ends downward.

Working in batches if necessary, put the mango purée in a blender, add the ginger purée or juice, the syrup from the jar, and 1 cup ice water and blend well.

Add sugar to taste. Blend again, then add more ice water until the mixture is the texture of thin cream. (If it's too thick it falls to the bottom of the glass.)

Arrange champagne flutes on serving trays, then put 1 teaspoon of the mango mixture into each one. Add a small teaspoon of champagne, stir and set aside until your guests arrive. When they do, top up the glasses with champagne (twice, because they bubble like mad), then put a ginger toothpick across the top of each one and tell your guests it's a swizzle stick.

Your guests will want more, so have extra mango mixture at hand.

*Note: Ginger purée is sold in jars in some supermarkets. To make your own, cut 2 lb. fresh ginger into pieces about 2 inches long. Soak in water to cover for about 30 minutes, then peel. Transfer to a blender or mortar and pestle and work to a purée. You may need to add a little ice water. You can press the juice through a strainer, or freeze the pulp in ice cube trays and use in this and other recipes as needed. You'll need at least 4 cubes for this recipe.

134

Mint Mojito

Caribbean Mojitos are the coolest of all rum drinks—and I like them made with tequila too! Before serving, strain this drink through a fine-mesh strainer to remove all the pieces of chopped mint (it's the mint juice that gives it such an amazing color).

½ cup white rum

juice of 2 limes

2 tablespoons sugar or sugar syrup

leaves from a large bunch of mint

ice cubes

sparkling mineral water (optional)

mint sprigs and lime zest, to serve

Serves 2

Put the rum, lime juice, sugar or sugar syrup, mint leaves, and ice cubes in a blender, zap well, then strain into glasses half-filled with ice.

Serve straight or topped up with sparkling mineral water, with a sprig of mint and a curl of lime zest.

Frozen Margarita

Margaritas, frozen or otherwise, are everybody's favorite drink. I think dipping the rim of the glass in salt is optional, but the slice of lime definitely isn't.

⅓ cup freshly squeezed lime juice, plus extra for the glass

salt, for the glass

⅓ cup Triple Sec or Cointreau

½ cup tequila

crushed ice

1 lime, halved and finely sliced lengthwise, to serve

Serves 6

Upturn the rim of each glass in a saucer of lime juice, then in a second saucer of salt.

Put the lime juice, Triple Sec or Cointreau, and tequila into a blender with some crushed ice. Zap until frothy. The sound of the motor will suddenly change as the froth rises above the blades.

Pour into the chilled, salt-rimmed Margarita glasses and serve with a slice of lime.

Strawberry Margarita

The ultimate girly drink!

1 basket ripe strawberries (about 12)

1 cup tequila

1 tablespoon powdered sugar or superfine sugar

juice of 1 lime

1 tablespoon strawberry syrup

crushed ice

Serves 6

Put all the ingredients in a blender with crushed ice. Blend and serve as in the previous recipe.

California Pineapple Tequila

It started in California, but now this is a favorite wherever there's sun and surf.

1 cup fresh pineapple juice

½ cup crushed ice

¼ cup golden tequila

Serves 2

Put all the ingredients in a cocktail shaker, shake, then strain into glasses full of ice cubes.

Swedish Glögg

Glögg is the Scandinavian version of glühwein or mulled wine—I much prefer it.

2 bottles dry red wine (750 ml each)

1 bottle aquavit or vodka (750 ml)

12 cardamom pods, crushed

8 whole cloves

1 orange

1 inch fresh ginger, sliced

1 cinnamon stick

1⅔ cups sugar, or to taste

1⅓ cups blanched almonds*

1¼ cups raisins*

cinnamon sticks, for stirring (optional)

Serves about 20

Using a vegetable peeler or canelle knife, remove the peel from the orange in a single curl (do not include any of the bitter white pith).

Put everything except the almonds and the cinnamon sticks in a bowl or non-reactive saucepan and set aside overnight (at least 12 hours).

Just before serving, heat to just below boiling point, then remove from the heat and stir in the almonds. Do not let boil or the alcohol will be burned off.

Serve in glass punch cups or tea glasses, with little spoons so people can scoop out the almonds and raisins. Small cinnamon sticks make delicious, scented stirrers.

*Note: If you prefer, omit the almonds and strain out the raisins before serving.

Children's Glögg

Why should children have all the fun? This is wonderful for non-imbibing adults as well.

1 orange

4 cups apple cider (non-alcoholic)

2 cups apple juice

5 tablespoons sugar

1 cinnamon stick

5 whole cloves

½ cup raisins*

Serves 10

Using a canelle knife or vegetable peeler, cut off the orange peel (not the biiter white pith) in a single curl.

Put the orange peel and all the other ingredients in a large non-reactive saucepan. Cover and set aside for 4 hours or overnight.

Just before the party, bring slowly to a boil over a gentle heat, then reduce to low and simmer for 30 minutes. Serve in punch cups or demitasse coffee cups, with some raisins and almonds in each serving.

*Note: The raisins can be strained out before serving if preferred. Traditionally this recipe also contains slivered almonds: I have omitted them because some children are allergic to nuts. If you like, share ¾ cup between the cups before serving.

Pimms

This traditional English summertime drink is perfect for parties. When borage is in flower, freeze the pretty blue blossoms in ice cubes for out-of-season Pimms drinks. Allow 1 cup per drink, and at least 2 drinks per person—but be prepared for repeat orders!

1 part Pimms

3 parts gingerale, lemonade, or soda

borage flowers

curls of cucumber peel

sliced lemons

sprigs of mint

Serves 1 or a party

Put all ingredients into a pitcher of ice, stir, and serve.

Ruby Grapefruit with Campari

Wonderful for a summer party—one glass per person as a welcoming drink. Campari at this level of dilution isn't very intoxicating, so this is a perfect drink for early in the day.

4 cups ruby grapefruit juice, chilled

½ cup Campari, or to taste

1 cup crushed ice, plus extra to serve

sprigs of mint, to serve

Serves 8–10

Put the grapefruit juice, Campari, and crushed ice in a blender and zap briefly. Half-fill a pitcher with more crushed ice and pour in the mixture. Cram lots of mint sprigs into the top of the pitcher, then serve.

Blue Champagne

Spectacularly cool, this is one you should only serve if you want your guests merry in seconds. Serve to the firstcomers—otherwise everyone will want one!

2 teaspoons freshly squeezed lemon juice

½ teaspoon Triple Sec or Cointreau*

½ teaspoon blue curaçao

½ cup vodka

champagne or other sparkling wine

Serves 2

Put ice cubes in a cocktail shaker, then add the lemon juice, Triple Sec or Cointreau, curaçao, and vodka.

Shake, then strain into 2 champagne flutes and top up with champagne.

Note: Triple Sec is best, but can be difficult to find. Use any dry orange-flavored liqueur instead—Cointreau is the most common.

Champagne Cocktail

There are other delicious champagne cocktails, all variations on the popular kir.

1 teaspoon of a liqueur such as Poire William, peach or strawberry liqueur, framboise, Midori, blue curaçao or Galliano and the pulp of 1 passionfruit

alternatively, ¼ cup fruit juice, such as pear, pineapple, peach, or apricot

champagne or other sparkling wine

Serves 1

Put 1 teaspoon of liqueur or ¼ cup fruit juice in a champagne flute or coupé and top with champagne.

Note: The glass is sometimes decorated with a slice of the fruit concerned.

139

Cranberry Cooler

Cranberry mixed with citrus juice is a marriage made in heaven—the prettiest, cloudy pink. It's great with vodka in a Sea Breeze, but this soft version is irresistible too.

4 cups cranberry juice

4 cups orange juice

ice cubes

sparkling mineral water

twists of orange peel, to serve

Serves 20

Mix the cranberry and orange juices in a pitcher.

Put the ice in tall glasses, half-fill with the cranberry mixture and stir well. Top with sparkling mineral water and serve with a twist of orange peel.

Soft Tropical Sangria

A non-alcoholic version of the traditional wine-based sangria, but with a South American twist. Use any fruit, but include tropicals, like mango, pineapple, or starfruit. Don't use any that go "furry," such as melon, kiwifruit, or strawberries. Wonderful for a summer party in the garden.

1 ripe mango, finely sliced

1 lime, finely sliced

1 lemon, finely sliced

½ pineapple, cut lengthwise into 6–8 wedges, then finely sliced to form triangles

1 starfruit (carambola), sliced

3 tablespoons sugar

8 cups gingerale or lemonade, well chilled

Serves about 12

Put the sliced fruit into a punch bowl. Sprinkle with sugar and set aside for at least 30 minutes. Top with icy gingerale or lemonade just before serving. Fill wine glasses with ice, add a few pieces of the fruit, then top with the fizzy liquid.

Variation: Peachy Sangria
Put 2 cups peach nectar, mint sprigs, and 2 sliced peaches in the bowl and top with gingerale or lemonade (or champagne).

Rock Shandy

Pretty and delicious. Bitters is high in alcohol, and though it is very much diluted in this drink, it's still there, and should not be served to people who never touch alcohol.

ice cubes

4 cups sparkling mineral water

Angostura bitters, to taste

sprigs of mint, to serve (optional)

Serves about 10

Fill 10 tall glasses with ice cubes, top with chilled sparkling mineral water and a sprig of mint. Add ½ teaspoon Angostura bitters to each glass—do not stir. The pink bitters will gradually sink to the bottom of the glass.

Choose a Menu

Summer Party

Ice-Cold Prairie Oysters
Spoonfuls of Spicy Thai Salad
Gazpacho
Flat Beans with Hummus
Mini Pizzas
Anchovy Pinwheels
Sushi Allsorts
Leaves with Baba Ganoush and
  Sesame Seeds
Fresh Vietnamese Spring Rolls
Lemongrass Sticks
Spiced Fresh Fruit
Gelati in Spoons or Brioche

142

Christmas Party

Spiced Nuts
Oven-Baked Tomatoes
Blini
Bruschetta and Pizzas
Asparagus and Pancetta Tartlets
Stuffed Vine Leaves
Turkey and Cranberry Leaf Wraps
Samosas
Tandoori Chicken
Middle Eastern Lamb Boats
Mini Christmas Cakes
Mini Croissants with Mincemeat
  and Brandy Cream

Winter Party

Pea Soup with Mint
Eggs with Dipping Sauce
Yunnan Spiced Spuds
Mini Hot Dogs with Mustard
Bruschetta and Pizza
Spicy Mini Shortbreads
Hummus Salad in Crisp Leaves
Smoked Chicken and Mexican Salsa
  in Leaf Wrap
Empanaditas
Mini Croissants with Mincemeat
  and Brandy Cream

Celebration Party

Spoonfuls of Caviar
Oysters on Ice
Plunged Shrimp with Chili Mojo
Chili Corn Muffins with Goat Cheese
  and Bacon
Seafood Sushi
Leaves with Goat Cheese and
  Smoked Salmon
Chicken Souvlaki
Yakitori
Mini Christmas Cakes (as celebration
  cake)

Casual Party in the Garden

Fish and Chips
Chargrilled Asparagus
Mini Hamburgers and Hot Dogs
Blue Cheese, Pine Nuts, and Basil Tartlets
Sushi Allsorts
Roast Beef and Wasabi Mayonnaise
  in Ciabatta
Mini Tortilla Wraps
Indonesian Beef Satays
Gelati in Spoons or Brioche

Wedding Party

Spicy Caribbean Chips
Baby Potatoes with toppings
Danish Open Sandwiches
Mini Bagels
Leek and Feta Tartlets
Sushi Cones
Thai Crab Salad in Endive Leaves
Crispy Pork Wontons
Tandoori Chicken
Mini Christmas Cakes (as wedding
  cake)

Vegetarian Menu

Sweet Potato Soup
Plantain Chips
Baby Potatoes with cream cheese
  and chives
Spanish Potato Tortilla
Cucumber Canapés
Bruschetta with Vegetable Toppings
Leek and Feta Tartlets
Potato Curry Cones
Cucumber Sushi
Stuffed Grape Leaves
Gelati in Spoons or in Brioche
Christmas Cakes

Any Party, Any Time

Cheese Straws
Caribbean Chips
Bruschetta and Pizza
Anchovy Pinwheels
Mini Hot Dogs and Hamburgers
Mini Tartlets with various fillings
Sushi Allsorts
Mini Pita Pockets
Chinese Purses
Vietnamese Spring Rolls
Lamb Kabobs
Singapore Pork Satays
Mini Croissants with Mincemeat
  and Brandy Cream
Gelati in Spoons or Brioche

Index

143